MW00653021

OUTRIDER

POEMS

ESSAYS

INTERVIEWS

OUTRIDER

Anne Waldman

La Alameda Press   Albuquerque

Some of these pieces have appeared in *Bombay Gin, Shiny, Square One*, and *The American Poetry Review* and were first published by Elik Press, and Hot Whiskey Press. "Show You Out the Door" was published in a Whitman Hom(m)age 2005/1855 by Turtle Point Press, 2005. "Premises of Consciousness" appeared in *The Poem That Changed America: "Howl" Fifty Years Later*, edited by Jason Shinder, 2006.

With special thanks to Erik Anderson, and to Claudia Cannizzaro and Joseph Richey for help with transcription and translation for the "Revolution / Evolution" interview with Ernesto Cardenal. And to the Civitella Ranieri Center, and Bellagio Study and Conference Center — sites that allowed time and place for some of these writing projects.

To my spiritual partners in the Outrider journey: Reed Bye, Steven Taylor, Anselm Hollo, Bobbie Louise Hawkins, Max Regan, Lisa Birman — Onward.

Frontispiece photograph: *Gregory Corso, 4th of July picnic, Naropa, 1992.*
COURTESY OF NAROPA ARCHIVES

Printed on 100% post-consumer waste recycled paper in accordance with the Green Press Initiative. The mission of the Green Press Initiative is to work with publishers, industry, and authors to create paper-use transformations that will conserve natural resources and preserve endangered forests.

Library of Congress Cataloging-in-Publication Data

Waldman, Anne, 1945-
   Outrider : poems, essays, interviews / Anne Waldman.
   p. cm.
   ISBN-13: 978-1-888809-48-0 (alk. paper)
   ISBN-10: 1-888809-48-5 (alk. paper)
   I. Title.

   PS3573.A4215O98 2006
   818'.5409--dc22

                        2006029142

La Alameda Press
9636 Guadalupe Trail
Albuquerque, New Mexico 87114

PRINTED IN CANADA

CONTENTS

To Ammiel Alcalay
for the activist friendship, and shelter from the storms of Empire

Patriarchal poetry needed with weeded with seeded with payed it
with left it without it with me. When this you see give it to me.
Gertrude Stein

To breath again in our lives anarchistically.
Way in. Apparently it's continuous.
John Cage

. . . but gradually I began reading the work of others who seemed
to be moving along the same lines. Given this sense of a "hidden"
community of workers such as myself, I replaced "the story of
the Revolution" with "the story of turning to words."
Tina Darragh

When the middle 1960s came along I was feeling split, schizophrenic. The
war, what was happening to America, the brutality of the world. What kind
of a man am I sitting at home, reading magazines, going into frustrated fury
about everything and then going in to my studio to adjust a red to a blue?
Philip Guston

Anne Waldman and Ted Berrigan, Boulder, 1976
PHOTOGRAPH BY ANDREA CRAIG

Outrider

OUTRIDER is a line of demarcation. It's words-obsession for the honor, dignity of a mind ill at ease, restless, jumping from desk to orally standing-at-attention, examining itself. A maker of poetry. Parallel to many makers of many things.

Markers of poetry, what are they?

They seem to be places where some truth might hold.

Energy made of language with its attendant properties — speech, song, ideas, music, image, skills of dicing, cutting, arrangement, gesture.

They could be synaptic.

What is truth in this tabulation?

A material object with signs that harness energy.

Crevasses, crannies, cirques — poems as receptacles, places where energies take up residence.

And linger.

Poems standing in for poets.

Malingering.

Is poetry a profession in this act of architecture?

How much backward from your own death do you write?

Is poetry a profession?

Or is poetry a receptacle?

What is poetry's relationship to the composite world,
in the relative world?

In the absolute world?

Sitting outside the mosque, unable to enter.

Sitting outside the *chandi bentar*, unable to enter.

Sitting outside the Hindu temple, unable to enter.

Sitting outside the monolith, American governance,
unable to shatter its hold.

Sitting outside one's original nature, hard to get back.

A small church in Chiapas, dirt floor covered with pine needles.
Tall white candles blazing — hundreds of them. Are you welcome?

On the page. In the air. On the street.
Perhaps a view or caparisoned lifestyle?

Enter.

Is poetry as profession in crisis? That's the view of OUTRIDER.
It's a question. A view inside maker/marker/poetry inside a question.

How many markers a day to be poet?

What is a description of a poet in Vietnam?
Not so markedly different.

I have to say it's a tribal responsibility.

Where does poetry reside? Where do poets living or dead reside?

Inside an office with hours posted?

Is there an agenda?

Is there a bid? A wager?

What are your writing implements?

What are thoughts? Where do they go? How do they form?

What are the portals, the *ayatanas,* for this poetry-head-restless-in-
process-of-shaping-itself-through-language, wanting that to be
enough for a whole life, yet troubled in "economy," in "career,"
in "maintenance," in bad governance.

In obligatory rounds. In network with its participial "-ing."

OUTRIDER seeks as view, this OUTRIDER motif, a way into the poet's role in a creative world increasingly commodified.
That sounds resoundingly glib.

However.

Sometimes to burst, to "know."

Poems have never been ideal glib products.

Or advertisements for "progress."

What is a poem's worth?

What is a poet who labored degrees worth?

With pedigrees?

The point is: *what do poets know?*

How might they earn a wage for what they know.
Non-negotiable.

How many degrees south or north, east or west would you go for a task in poetry?

Horse latitudes.

How far would the instigating *topos* extend?

How much is a poet with accolades worth?

A poet with reputation's value?

A "celebrated poet" on the sliding slope of social speech.

Start again.

Where did poetry start streaming in a poet? That would be a starter.

Meaning that because a poem is historically quite a little product, what might you do except struggle to survive with a way you can continue making this thing not so valued monetarily. And being sustained in this making of no little thing, even divine.

Teach, scholar-poet with Knowledge to "impart."

This is serious. And how I have adored my students.

In exchange for health insurance, retirement benefits. Ha!

Library.

Worry the essential library.

Write what you would want to read.

Utopian poetics, what you want to read.

How to play.

Start with poem as career. Perhaps, ideally, where poetry presents,
offers, little product value . . . It inculcates "a way into,"
it is a process of becoming shapely, of becoming mind/language/
imagination/music shape-of — what form could that be, how might
a semantics hold all this?

Or philosophy? *Against the grain* of closure, perhaps . . .

It — the path as practiced by forebears — informs our entire history,
being outside the mainstream (the prevailing trend of opinion,
fashion . . .), eschewing rhetoric, piety, ambition, reward . . .

Progress? Avant-derrière?

One feels agelessly hooked up to "other." Sappho for her gnomic mystery,
Dickinson for her gnomic imagery, Gertrude Stein, H.D., Mina Loy,
Lorine Niedecker are in the conversations in a random gnomic head.

Historical precedence surely. OUTRIDER as a term, a concept, a battle cry
(because one is a warrior in 1974) is born in 1974 at The Jack Kerouac
School of Disembodied Poetics, Naropa Institute (later University).
It's a wild mind experiment.

Wild mind: elegantly self-disciplined.

The etiquette of poetic freedom.

Step gently on the earth.

"Institute," they (the bank tellers) would look at you funny if the checks were bouncing, checks issued by the mad house, the "institute."

Where do you go? You wake up one morning as a poet prohibited by job, desk, stationery, economics.

No desk, no telephone, no stationery, no accreditation.

A good idea: Contemplative education. Non-competitive education.

Then comes threat of standardization. Institutionalization.

The struggles for a new idea for a place of poetry at The Kerouac School to define this program's pedagogy in a present increasingly debilitated by concerns of economics, professionalism, demands of young writers who arrive as "clients" with a perceived need to be satisfied, assuaged, are problematic.

And they are paying clients and some of them are brilliant.

At the turn of the century you worry some will not hold the vision, will abuse it. Aggression you say it so, and ego and fear.

But the Ur-project/experiment is more magical than that and how to get it back?

Who carries it forward?

Other spheres, rooms for conversation.

It's a different time. Some people died. Something needed to survive.

Needed micro-management?

Doubt this.

The Summer Writing Program trying to carry the initial vision forward.
Because it sees the temporary autonomous zone, the utopian zone,
a Zen zone, that won't be institutionalized.

From 1974 to the present, and it's a fair exchange in dollars.
The question is: Is it?

What are the models of apprenticeship?

How is the call heard? First it is heard. A line somewhere? Propensity.
It is available, this view, this *modus*, in response and as an alternative to
poetry as a career. Or of at least *thinking of it that way*. Operating in it —
the composition by rhizome field — that way, as if poetry is an excursion
and a necessity.

Where is our poetry today? Where does it come from?
From where we cannot see and might never venture to?

The philosophers still talk about Nerval, Rimbaud, Artaud,
Shakespeare, luminaries from a familiar canon.

Where is Frank O'Hara? Charles Olson? Robert Duncan? Ed Dorn?
Robert Creeley so recent in his grave?

Where is Allen Ginsberg now? Waiting in the bardo to take re-birth?
Enjoying the 50th anniversary of *Howl*?

So many poetry histories/cultures since then.

What to be said about the new and emerging poetry cultures way
beyond the New American Poetry?

[French *carriere* from Italian *carriera*
from Provençal *carreira* from Latin *carrus*.]

Literally: A racecourse.

Literally: A short gallop of a horse at full speed; a charge,
an encounter on horseback.

Literally: A swift running course; an act of careening;
full speed, impetus.

A course or progress through life or history; an occupation or
profession engaged in as a life-work; a way of making a livelihood
and advancing oneself.

Should poets be paid for what they do? Should they be housed and
fed for their dulcet sound? Sing for their supper?

And it might be ghostly or tangible as it rides and crests, existing
as the requisite line of words, of thought-in-words, of pictures-in-
words. Action. A tradition made up on the spot. Sine waves, air waves.
Projected. Proclamation.

You won't be alienated. Would you recognize yourself as one of them?

The line to pull you in, to save your life. What category is your storm?

How do you differ? Ritually? Metaphysically?

What is the story? Is it a calling or a career?

How do you ride? Sidesaddle. Saddle-less?

Is the metaphor one of manifest destiny or of cultural intervention?

Colonized?

Of cavalry. Let's destroy the wild west once and for all and learn something about manifest density.

A woman rides with her hair on fire.

A western predilection, all those fitful cowboy/indian movies.

Vaqueros, Native warriors. Gauchos, sharpshooters. Indian Chiefs wait for reclamation tense in history.

Can you exist without the road, the company (compañeros, compañeras), without a map of the world?

Without a compass?

What is the sexuality of the poetics of OUTRIDER?

That's just it. Invoking the notion of "coming out," of being outed, of being outside the norm.

Recognizing the linear body, lunar body, illuminated body, liminal body. Body poetics.

Transgressed, trans-gendered.

Or body maimed in war. Body scarred many ways.

Body politic. Afflicted body politic.

Crossing the line of scrimmage.

Without the oral tradition, shout and moan, could (might) you be heard?

I thought of a tsunami.

Water that moves mountains.

Destruction, danger, death. Suffering.

The effect of our response, or lack of.

The inability to imagine. Visualize Other.

Poet's gift: Other.

The poet's duty is to move the century forward a few inches towards Other.

Toward the Human.

"I is a human universe."

Risk burden onus.

Charm.

Citizen.

Are you a citizen or a refugee?

When you take refuge in Buddhism you give up attachment to personal history. Break the chain — *rahula*.
The name of Sakyamuni Buddha's son — *Rahula*.

Many images light up: you heard about attachment. Do you break off from the tree (as in lineage tree or tree of knowledge), become a ragged text without a common margin. Human with an asymmetrical gait. Handmade. A tree seared in the brain, how many branches will hold the things you do & hope to do.

Gate with paper keys to the garden. Self-secret garden.

"And the gates of this chapel were shut and 'thou shalt not' writ over the door . . ."

A map of the US of America, "thou shalt not."

So what may we do, poets? Or not do.

The old invisible one that is not one America is exposed.

Remember the others of the American continent.

Where you might work in shadow in your subterranean plot
"to keep the world safe for poetry."

Split. Spilt.

Blood. Of the poet.

What line of demarcation?

One who rides outside the normative strategy, who will brook
no obstacle to the next kinetic moment.

Colorful tattered bodhisattvas. With saddlebags, words at the
center of mind, never banish thinking of Other.

For the benefit of others. You take them with you into the audience
and psyche of poem.

OUTRIDER even likes others' poetry too, buys the books of others.

Maker of books she might be. Maker of schools.

Realist. How do we change the frequency of commodified world?

Fantasist.

The path less traveled. Least. Lease or ransom.
Blue stocking for pithy imagination.

She had a yen for the outside . . . trapped in a mindset
of "prison" all day.

It had no boundaries being so out in "the open."

Is it possible to train in this? one asked.

The most snarling environmental disaster could move you to action. *Train
in disaster.*

When they euphemistically began the war on terror, you, as poet,
felt inadequate to the struggle for language. Yet.

Follow by inclination and example those others who also, by
inclination, felt poetry the rival government.

Who is fragile by nature, and defined as pulse, as frequency. And in the
realm of accountability as palpable, trustworthy, and moreover painted in
this tableau as ageless, a deathless comrade. Okay, let's
admit a state of mind.

Come into the House of the Mother. Antechamber. Scriptorium.
Out on the street. Are you ready for the Free University?

Privilege a state of mind.

Beyond race, class, gender.

With or without a horse, a mount, an infrastructure.

Back to animal mount, animalize spirit.
The poem is not a little machine in this installation.

The randomness and inter-connectedness of the rhizome
was already invoked.

Input from all directions. Sanskrit: *pratitya-samutpada.*

What survives of the bomb shelter?

Are the wild animals permitted inside?

And who in an open system?

Come out, you can come out now.

Who do you serve?

The poem is not a calvary rescuing the masses.

When you saw — & the world cried "shame! shame!" —
the fate of the survivors of the *huracán* (from Carib *furacan*),
and those you would see who didn't make it, what did you think?

What was your rage? Is your rage. Katrina: Every second thought.

Ancient of days. A rune, a trick of a writing hand, a cultural
intervention. Left-handed. Voice that isn't necessarily heard.
Hiding in the brush, just bumbling down to the shore for a look . . .

Do you face the East? Is China out there and enticing?

Is China the new cyborg-ian "enemy?"

Who you, dear child of OUTRIDER, will serve financial debt to?

Alone but not lonely.

As.

Socratic when necessary.

Dialectics to argue the point.

As.

Not a biblical revelation, not a jihadist or angel of doom.

Message from the East, you happened to be listening.

The bodhisattva vow.

Do well to encourage children to read poetry with flashlights under the
sheets into the late night, sans souci dawn.

Encourage street corner culture. What happens below the radar.

New Orleans culture, for example, created on the street.

What OUTRIDER desires is a return to urgency for the work
because we are trying to wake up the awareness of the world.

Not in a safer academy, although maybe help from there would come.

Help, come soon.

Below the economic radar.

Help, come soon.

Speak to "thirsty," speak to "homeless."

Words are inadequate often to experience.

But to imagination?

You have to think skillfully about how best to help
other sentient beings.

Going to war won't help, especially if you are the invader.

I understand although loathe the oppressor motivated by power, by
greed but why is he (it's usually a he) so sadistic?

Is this genetic?

Is poetry a genetic propensity?

Is enlightenment a genetic ?

"Can a thing like this — writing poetry — be taught?"

How many got their start in school?

Nor corporate or banal evil-doer be.

The nature guardians are not happy about global warming.
Messages from the phenomenal world.

OUTRIDER will listen and keep a record, scribed indelibly in water
in sand, in a saddlebag with items of regret.

Mementos of a reckless century: empty water bottle,
crust of bread, dried meat, rock salt.

A small notepad with a message to all survivors.

What we need, O OUTRIDERS, is the modality of compassion.

Take no hostages here.

Release the devil in you who works overtime.

OUTRIDER might circumambulate a mountain.

Moment: Redolent of change. Life and death of . . .
giving expectations a rest.

Moment: Nowhere to go again but the library.

Into thick and inquisitive repositories of sense.

Sound? Sense? Curiosity?

Sundered reticence?

A popular song with no closure is familiar to OUTRIDER.

Gasoline prices up.

It is a blue line, a red line, a black line.

A musical signature.

It is a white line, a yellow line, a green line. It is less evident in
consideration of a lawn. Or a byline. A graveyard.

It is a no fly zone at times, it is a demilitarized zone at other times.

It connotes a cave sculpted by wind, hollow or occupied.
In which a mark was made in expectation of eternity.

OUTRIDER: At the cusp.

And I was heartened to see — on the streets of New York
at many a protest — writers of all dispositions who would not have
been speaking before the war.

What does it take in the genetic nucleosomic-human-animal-plant
universe to muster "change?"

With gene of pig, with gene of monkey. With gene of a snow pea.

A wrathful deity rides her mount.

OUTRIDER is a hybrid.

OUTRIDER is a witness and an animal-plant-mineral-citizen, and
strives to make change in the realm of inclusion, inasmuch
as OUTRIDER can be persuasive, and inclusion might be a goal.
Inclusion in what? The discourse.

In the Open.

Of talking, gesturing about sanity.

Might they be colleagues in a shakedown for Poetry
as Rival Government?

A stance is required that sets apart, yet co-exists with the notion
of a poetry of risk (sanity) and surprise (language).

It would take a kind of magic perhaps to persuade you of
the enormity of OUTRIDER's task. It is felt to be urgent and
unregulated yet it can make no harm or wage no bodily occupation.

OUTRIDER is not a Psy-Ops.

It is a term we used to fire your mind.

It can shape-shift, but usually away from official, standard, middle, mediocre, solutions of imagination and language.

Imago.

Pluperfect.

A ghost behind the first and last "lines," "sentences."

One phoneme too often.

Or lines of response between outer, inner, and secret duty.

OUTRIDER is a declension of possibility. OUTRIDER claims the source to be a way of regarding the terrain, thus a View.

OUTRIDER is a statement about language and its purpose.

And the cries of animals.

To contend, to enliven, to distance, to advocate, to investigate, to rally, to prioritize, to surprise.

To take all the articles of faith and shake them down.

Not no ideas, but no ideas but in projectiles of things.

To vocalize. To mouth the impossible.

Present tense or pretense of the "moment."

To circumvent your notions of official (post-tribal) art.

Circle the wagons.

OUTRIDER is a documentarian. Old archivist of imagination.

Who gets the final cut?

What you might see and understand is the body in space, struggling with language.

What you might perhaps see is the scientific nature of change and choice.

What is your genetic proclivity? As mammal? As avian?

He was a big man (Charles Olson).

He was difficult, attentive, the best correspondent (James Schuyler).

He was a taut man (Robert Creeley).

He was an activity demon (Allen Ginsberg).

He was a funny man (Kenneth Koch).

He was a talking man (Robert Duncan).

He was an OUTRIDER (Ted Berrigan).

He was born *to live as variously as possible* (Frank O'Hara).

He was fragile and drawn to the flame (John Wieners).

He was a mystic (Jack Spicer).

These were men. *These were people who died.*

Once upon a time before the great and un-ending wars,
OUTRIDER was a hunter and gatherer. O'Hara was a sailor.

Once upon a time before the great and un-ending wars, OUTRIDER
considered the animals. Their habits, traits, beauty. Their habitats.

OUTRIDER wept.

OUTRIDER considered how they, the animals, might dream,
what their dream-shapes might be.

How many poet men served their country compared to now?

Patriarchal Poetry might be withstood.

Patriarchal Poetry or peace to return to Patriarchal Poetry
or pieces of Patriarchal Poetry.

How lucid could that be? Memories of fleeing, of being wounded.
Of being separated from the rest of the herd.

OUTRIDER foraged and came up to the present with a method of thinking and retrieval.

What could OUTRIDER not imagine?

She might have silver crescent moon spurs on her methodical boot.

Matrilinear boot.

Swamp lore.

Loot.

Attitude.

"Far out."

"Way out."

"Outed."

"Come out."

"Outsider."

"Outspoken."

"Outrage."

"Outburst."

"Outcry."

"Outlaw."

"Outlast."

"On the 'outs.'"

OUTRIDER is One that rides.

OUTRIDER is a person who rides horses.

OUTRIDER rides herd on.

OUTRIDER rides high.

A clause having little relevance to the main issue,
added to a legislative bill.

Something resting on or supported by something else.

Just let them re-write the Constitution, just let them. Hell to pay.

OUTRIDER would take on the Cavalry.

OUTRIDER: A mounted attendant who rides in front of or beside
a vehicle.

An escort. A scout.

How "out" might you go from the strictures of the
official verse realm?

How might you ride a vehicle of poetry?

OUTRIDER distinguishes between reality and simulacrum.

OUTRIDER wishes to appease your unease and posit "career" but can't.

Is this a line of demarcation?

Career is a twist, a synthetic solution.

Think you are, compañeros of my century, in a career?

OUTRIDER cannot consume its own theory.

Can the limits of my language define the limits of my world?

Are you writer-ly or readerly?

I read to write, I write to read, etc.

OUTRIDER will maintain an historical perspective, considering all
the tropes outside OUTRIDER-dom.

OUTRIDER obfuscates the message with another message: not operate
right down the middle, whatever that means. Golden medium.

Meridians in the body were thought to be rivulets.

I would go way left of center, but save us from leftist lingo.

There is mainstream, there are figures and you will know what they
say with what closure they milk it, figures like mouths, like persons
who have a public mouth, gorgeous spokespersons.

Some responsibility with a public mouth. I will not advertise any
of your glow or identity, think for yourself with public mouth,
the good of the whole is what is mouthed one would hope.

The same old struggle between the proletariat and the bourgeoisie.

Be careful bourgeoisie of poetry, be careful.

Be prepared to go underground.

Bourgeoisie creating its own destruction.

Naked self interest. Cash nexus.

I guzzle fossil fuel.

OUTRIDER might throw in the towel.

Tropes of flood. Hyper-reality of flood.

You wrap your mind to it and say "biblical proportions."

Robin Hood as OUTRIDER. Tithe the rich.

Warp and woof of the economy.

Tithed time becomes you.

I want to make something inspired by nothing foregrounded at all.

The page becomes a terrain, an abode, a mystical site.

OUTRIDER is feeling a person an historical perspective.

OUTRIDER is an endangered species.

OUTRIDER is not progress in an art or poetics
but OUTRIDER is progress.

Outrider: The Pedagogy

Definition

"OUTRIDER" was a term some of us adopted early on at the inception of The Jack Kerouac School of Disembodied Poetics at Naropa University (then Naropa Institute) in Boulder, Colorado. Co-founder Allen Ginsberg had his own generation's terms and identifications. I felt the need to define the lineage, pedagogy and view of a burgeoning poetics program that was increasingly seeing itself outside the official verse literati culture academic mainstream. And capture, poetically, impetuously, the *zeitgeist* of that program. Dick Gallup used the term OUTRIDER for a class on the New York School. New York School as defined by Edwin Denby was non-provincial. Ed Dorn's *Gunslinger* was in the mix. We were situated close to the Continental Divide, near the tundra that conjoined East and West and its dramatic powerful run-offs. Clear to the Pacific and Atlantic. The New American Poetry and its outer reaches were the prerequisite "lineage." The Jack Kerouac School of Disembodied Poetics, although positing and realizing a "body poetics," for years had no office, had no telephone, no typewriter, no stationery, no handsome desks, no library. This had a sweet resonance with the Prajna Paramita Sutra: no eyes, no ears, no mind. In the mix also: Tantric Tibetan with its notion of "crazy wisdom," a subtle and rigorous study of mind. We sought to provide a cohesive structure for a community and its offspring that had come of age during the Vietnam War years, and had been actively part of the struggle for civil rights, women's rights, gay rights. "Come study with people who have been jailed for their beliefs." This seemed a counter-poetics resistant to, *au rebours* "institutionalization" of creative writing. That resisted the micro-management of a standardized model. That could invent itself and was invited to enter the Buddhist mandala and do just that. That resisted the domination of the literary mafias of New York and Chicago and San Francisco. That could feed off the various hybrids of the New American Poetry. That could take the project further. As a *temporary autonomous zone* (Hakim Bey's phrase). As a bohemian community. The economics were a challenge. Students arriving somewhat randomly were a challenge. The Institute is now a university and properly accredited. What gets lost?

A curious amalgam then, an open system then.

And now: Survival. Whatever it takes.

It was a second generation away from the New American Poetry with its branches of Beat, Black Mountain, New York School and San Francisco Renaissance. Umbra in the mix.

Plurality

Plurality as a Poetics: Begins with a series of questions. What are the implications of the new information world? How will we manage our diminishing fossil fuel? Our diminishing civil liberties? Who will be "in charge?" What are the shifting paradigms the world faces? What is the New World Order that seeks to control whole populaces, governments, theocracies, plutocracies? May an artist, in fact, create, muster energy toward an act of beauty after atrocity? What is the ignorance about history that does not face the truth of its own karmic nightmare? Or does not experience the urgency of the call to struggle for peace, justice, humanity? How may poets — privileged, educated, or autodidact — relieve the suffering of "other," of "others?" How does one respond on behalf of other? What is the "other" in us? The plurality in us? After 9/11 Arundhati Roy said to the US of America: "Welcome to the world." The charnel ground of Ground Zero with its amalgam of individuals of copious background was extremely vivid in its plurality. It also showed the way that people, whether they realize it or not, are working in tandem with others, in fact they may be working at jobs that are contributing to the suffering of others. The destructions brought to mind the killing fields of Cambodia, the slaughter of Rwanda, Srebrenica, and images of conflict everywhere, elsewhere, *over there*. Lebanon.

"The sacrificed others" in Jean Baudrillard's sense perhaps?

The brutal violence in countless "other" — realities go abstract, for the most part, in the American mind. But it also created a backlash, a desperate sense of revenge. What a rare opportunity to wake up, in fact, to become part of the world — instead it was used as an excuse, for America, in its own suspect and illegitimate governance, to become more isolated, more ignorant, more arrogant, more barbaric, more greedy.

Many millions have protested the wars in Afghanistan and Iraq. This latest war (this "eternal war") has shown people are connected in their struggle now "more" than ever before. I found myself in contact constantly with others all over the world in protest. And I found myself writing letters of protest to the embassies of other countries. Yet there is a kind of death wish in the land as a child in Africa dies of malaria every 30 seconds. As the weaponry created for "the eternal war scenario" grows crueler — the horrific "daisy cutter" that slashes apart its victims with incredible and un-bearable pressure and brutality. The psychological suffering, in fact the "wounded psyche" all around is papable. WHAT IS THIS TO POETRY?

Post-traumatic stress syndrome is palpable. Our dreams and nightmares vent our fear and confusion all the time. This is a little report on one of the workers in the aftermath of ground zero in November 2001 (when they are still sifting through body parts): "If I had people in here, I'd want to know someone was looking too," Danny Nolan says. He has night-mares now, waking up screaming about the job sometimes. Friends from the past who have died visit him, like the old friends whose names he will not speak because of the belief that the name now belongs only to the soul. In the dream, the friend takes him into a strange room and shows him actual items that Mr. Nolan has seen recovered from the World Trade Center, things like African artifacts. "The place is playing tricks on me, I guess."

There is a plurality of the mind, of the imagination.

There is a sense of plurality vs. dominance.
The US of A is the single largest producer of greenhouse emissions, generating twenty percent of the global total.

Who rules and why?

Could Henry Kissinger ever be brought to trial for the secret bombing of Cambodia? Could Ariel Sharon in absentia be brought to trial for the massacre of Palestinians in Lebanese refugee camps? How many generations for the Hutu & Tutsi to find resolution and so on. How many generations for Iraqis to forgive the perpetrators of their unmitigated suffering?

How does a poetics take on so much wanton killing?

Nearly 400 billion in the Pentagon budget that proposes cleaner — even more unmanned — "weapons of mass destruction." We have our Yucca Mountain in the US — a volcanic ridge in the desert 100 miles North-west of Las Vegas as the current favored burial spot for radioactive waste, which will be dangerously radioactive for hundreds of thousands of years.

A report indicated with some satisfaction that leakage will be strictly limited to 10,000 years! The movies and media continue to glamorize war. One most egregious example, the movie *Black Hawk Down*, re-counts the US Special Forces action in Mogadishu, in which eighteen Americans died and several thousand Somalians. The characters refer to the Somalians as "skinnies." You see the same computerized shot of the abstracted "other" over and over again — the "skinny" being hit and crumbling. There's a strange sadism here. There's the "manufacturing of consent" in Noam Chomsky's term that can persuade. The oft-repeated degraded images of Iraqi people looting and pillaging — another example of the de-humanizing agenda of corporate-media-thug rule.

More recently it comes unglued.

The planet itself — the fragile eco-system, which contains multiple plu-
ralities, trembles underfoot and is trembling to a greater degree as the
smoke of shock and awe clears. Where is our "Practice of the Wild?"
Where is the etiquette of human and "other?" Toward all the denizens,
pluralities of the world. The world is listing as we consume more and
more baubles and create more weapons of mass destruction.

Where does OUTRIDER see OUTRIDER in the rest of the world?

In prison.

Trapped.

I've been fortunate in recent years to have traveled and lived in several less
consumer-istic communities outside my own communities of New York
and Boulder. But I've had the occasion to work abroad — particularly in
Indonesia, where I've been a participant and student primarily in Bali —
studying philosophy, religion, and the arts and politics, including the
gamelan *gong kebyar* with its interlocking cycles of bursting sound. And
organizing poetry events with local writers.

How to get back there now? To Java? To Sumatra? The US State
Department issues strong advisories for Americans — and others who
support them — albeit westerners — all viewed as symbols of Empire
and targets for extremism.

•

Students — during a recent manifestation of a performance class I've taught at Naropa University entitled "Liberation Now!" — fretted over the cultural imperialism and colonialism of Antonin Artaud and Ezra Pound. Their respective white privileged "gaze" toward Balinese and Tarahumara cultures in the case of Artaud (although Artaud travelled to Mexico to live and ritually ingest peyote with these peoples), and Japanese Noh in the case of Pound. Is mere literary "orientalism," an old trope, the problem here? I gave some historical context that, while not trying to beg the issues particularly, gave weight to these writers' important acts of exploration. William Carlos Williams' "Beautiful Thing" had also recently been called into question in its objectification of women. Ted Berrigan's use of the word "legs," and so on. Could Gertrude Stein's own anti-semitism be seen perhaps as "internalized oppression?" The privilege (of "not having to work a day job") of H.D., incipient racism of many of the moderns. Charles Olson's use of the word "chink." The class and privilege and academia-cizing of so many of the Language Poets and so on. What arose, also, was a sense of the real "split" in the culture so obvious in the recent Presidential elections' debacles where many people of color were disenfranchised and where blue-collar-white-male-ethos was undervalued in terms of the weight it carries toward a conservative (and scary) agenda. Not to mention the dysfunctionality of the party system and so on. Where is a writing and by extension, a performance, which includes a consideration of the whole "polis?" Impossible! one thinks. The examples of dismay are endless when much of the avant-garde reads as elitist, operating within very specific language and economic codes, and where the arenas are MLA conferences, literature and creative writing "departments," Barnes and Noble bookstores and the like. *Is being a poet now about being "tenured?"* one student laments.

The critiques are legion. The discussions of these and other matters seemed to delay looking (just one example) into the actual Noh plays (in translations of Pound and others), and there was understandable resistance to the idea of writing our own "version" of a Noh — a tall order in any case — and yet there have been many post-modern examples of Noh-inspired performance. As one student gave a recent presentation on the Songlines of the Australian aborigines, another student shuddered with fear that we shouldn't be hearing about these sacred practices lest it further exposed the aborigines to exploitation and decimation.

I appreciate the inquiry and sensitivity to any act of investigation of "other." How is "performance" beholden to the past? What does the act of bringing text to gesture to vocalization or multi-vocalizations have to do with ritual, with rite? With "literature" of the past, for that matter? What blurring occurs in creative work? Must pedagogy begin with disclaimer? With caution? Is this just an era of fashionable political correctness? Are we, as teachers/guides, here to defend, undo, re-configure, re-articulate, transgress? How does one cut through to the "real work," or are we so entwined with the confusions and mistakes of our so-called lineages that time must be spent in analyses, "processing" and correction? Who speaks for *me*? One trans-gendered student asks, *and, How dare they*? Yet ecological and cultural preservation and preservation of *the human* are some of the goals of the Naropa project as languages and all manner of plants and animals disappear daily. An urgent reclamation sometimes at odds with healing the psychic wounds so prevalent in people today — from all backgrounds of race, ethnicity, class, gender. I have declared in one manifesto, a writing beyond gender, and have tried to inspire a poet's Boddhisattva Vow, in which one becomes a bridge, a path, a shelter, *whatever is required*, for others. And one reads and studies and performs . . . for the benefit of others.

Sometimes I just go silent. Bohemian-artistic roots and view seem woefully anachronistic, inadequate.

OUTRIDER soars in me, where will OUTRIDER find her place?

Will generations hence look back at this time and see it as another Holocaust where we didn't take care of each other or our world? Where poets might have accomplished more in the area of human rights, in alleviating the suffering of the poor and impoverished. Think about it.

As of this writing 55,000 dead in Pakistan, the toll rising. Three million people without shelter. And Darfur.

•

The Naropa University in Boulder, Colorado is named for the 11th century Buddhist Indian pandit and yogin Naropa, who was the abbot of the historic Nalanda University, now a ruin site in Bihar State, India. Naropa University was founded in 1974 by a Tibetan Buddhist lama, Chogyam Trungpa, and some of his principal students, which included poets. These were disaffected, some dissident folk, some who had been particularly active in the turbulent sixties as political and cultural activists.

Trungpa and others felt the need for an alternative mode of education that would actualize a contemplative, non-competitive and mutually-supporting atmosphere blending America and Western traditions of practice and scholarship with Buddhism and other wisdom traditions, including Native American indigenous traditions. The Arts were to be in the foreground, perceived as ultimate "crazy wisdom" (outrageous, unpredictable) practices — the quick path to enlightenment, or chaos?

Community service and "outreach" were seen as important activities and a balance to the chaotic, personally investigative side that art and spiritual practice demands. One could be trained to help the world. And live one's life in sane and meaningful ways not based on monetary or worldly gain. A school arming its students with ideas of how to ease the pain of suffering seemed radical in 1974.

The Boddhisattva Vow involves a practice of *tonglen*, or sending and receiving practice in which the pratictioner takes on — visually, emotionally — the suffering of others. Allen Ginsberg spoke of this time (late 20th century) being a time of grieving, and of "trying the human" — "everything else/drunken dumbshow." He chose a poetry of witness. Amiri Baraka in his many visits to Naropa always invokes "the struggle." Being situated practically next door to Rocky Flats plutonium plant (still the most toxic site in the US, deemed now a "closure project" with final waste removed and now on the move through New Mexico, although portions of the site where plutonium leaked into the soil remain a danger as of October, 2005) allowed a meditative awareness to permeate one's entire existence along the Colorado front range. An acute sense of the larger picture was/is always present. Cold facts of wrong-headedly induced risk. Unmitigated ignorance that continues as I write this where the governing political covenant is suggesting more nuclear power plants for the nation, bowing to the hegemony of big business and the inevitable karma of wanton environmental desecration.

John Cage, Allen Ginsberg, Diane di Prima, Jackson McLow and others present the first summer when we founded the Poetics School felt a link to the Black Mountain experiment and to the Zen teachings of D.T. Suzuki and others, which had radicalized their own thinking and the thinking of many avant-garde artists of the last century.

Sierra Collom, Jack Collom, Robert Creeley, Allen Ginsberg, Anne Waldman,
Philip Whalen (left to right) in the parking lot, Naropa, 1984
PHOTOGRAPH BY PETER ORLOVSKY

John Cage unequivocally stated that Black Mountain took place "at lunch," a metaphor surely for a sense of community, an exchange that didn't need formal parameters but extended, happily, beyond the classroom.

At an early meeting when the poets were invited to help design a poetics component for the school, Trungpa casually remarked that Naropa was going to be "a hundred year project, at least," which, for all of us, communicated the necessity of designing something worthwhile for future generations. It wasn't just about creating a cozy little scene for ourselves, however fruitful that might be. Allen Ginsberg and I arrived at the name

Summer Writing Program, Naropa, 1992 — students with assorted faculty:
Joanne Kyger, Anselm Hollo, Donald Guravich, Bobbie Louise Hawkins,
Anne Waldman, Allen Ginsberg, Andrew Schelling
PHOTOGRAPH COURTESY OF NAROPA ARCHIVES

The Jack Kerouac School of Disembodied Poetics with a sense that
Kerouac had exemplified the First Buddhist Noble Truth, being the Truth
of Suffering. Kerouac had trusted his spontaneous mind, although this
didn't mean he would not revise his writing, and had authored some of
the most provocative and unique literature — prose and poetry both —
in the 20th century. A complicated mongrel mix (Quebecois-American)

he was the quintessential restless, talented, displaced "seeker." "Satori," or the blast that comes from a flash of recognition of human and planetary frailty, was experienced in his case outside the usual "epiphany" you find in subject-matter poetry. We wanted something vital, difficult outside the official verse culture academic mainstream. Would this be it? Satori!

We were also part of a continuum of writers and thinkers no longer alive. Allen, at times, was taking his directives from William Blake. Hearing voices.

Book Liberation Day

One, as writer, is guided by text as one hears it at the moment of com-
position, a process which may obviously be refined. Performance is an
act or rite re-done. This extends to transgressing the boundaries of offi-
cial performance/theater/gallery/museum/reading spaces and interven-
ing in unexpected ways where people may be forced to encounter new
social conventions, re-orderings in the art/life conundrum. It was inter-
esting to organize a large class of students — we had on-site classes
around the town of Boulder, including one session by the Arapahoe
Creek where we discussed Stein's kinesthetic experiments with writing
outdoors, resulting in one case, as she wrote by water in the novel *Lucy
Church Amiably* — to transgressive, albeit gentle, acts of intervention.
Reading out loud to the rhythms of the natural world. How do they
compute with reading aloud surrounded by unnatural rhythms or with
our own psycho/physical patternings in our own, very distinct nervous
systems? What buzz rides there?

We decided to declare a Book Liberation Day for which we amassed
quite a few tomes to liberate — getting text off the page and into the ear,
as well as liberating a book from a dusty shelf — and then to read from,
approaching (attacking?) particular people who seemed lost in their dis-
traction gadgets: cell phones, computers, "pals," headsets and so forth. We
would sidle up to an ear and begin our readings. I found modulating my
voice from whisper to song to shout was effective. A choice of William
Blake's "America A Prophecy" seemed particularly apt: "The shadowy
daughter of Urthona stood before red Orc./ When fourteen suns had
faintly journey'd o'er his dark abode;/His food she brought in iron bas-
kets. His drink in cups of iron." Was I a shadowy daughter on the safe mall
of Boulder? Was the "food" poetry? Imprisoned in its manacles of condi-

Anne Walman and Ed Sanders at the Frankfurt Book Fair, Germany, 1995
PHOTOGRAPH COURTESY OF IDE HINTZE AND DIE SCHULE FUR DICHTUNG

tioned response? *Poetry? It's toast,* one highschool kid had quipped at an Outreach session the week before. I'd show him . . . and yet it was the kids and the elders who stood respectfully listening to us as we intoned William Burroughs, Mina Loy, William Blake.

Among other things . . . Transmission is . . .

an auto-motive assembly of gears and associated parts by which power is transmitted from the engine to a driving axle. Also called a *gearbox.*

A sending across . . . an investigation of the intrinsic provisions of language that is passed on . . .

Observe the militarization of daily ordinary life ... *don't you want to say something about it to someone?*

There is a notion of "passing it on," that simple. One to one. Elder to younger perhaps. That "poetry is news," that the inspiration for any work you do and the work you do as a writer and artist connects you to an ageless continuum. "In the mind of the poet, all times are contemporaneous."

That a notion of a community sympathetic to this notion of passing it on exists. That you are not alone in your projective voice, in the arena of your various languages and cultures. That you write missives, that you might be on a mission, that you won't miss anything, that you are active, energetic, that language is imaginative through all the shapes and sizes of itself — trans, bi, straight, polysemous ...

You can force this stuff down people's throats but there's a creative gene in everyone's psyche. They need us reminding them and ourselves.

"I'll raise all the books of my poems over the heads of the creeps!" declaimed Tristan Tzara.

Awake out of your sloth! Get your life in gear! We DON'T want to be speaking the language of Empire, of Auschwitz.

Hybrid

How is OUTRIDER a hybrid?

I've been thinking about the hybrid cars — Toyota Prius, the Honda Civic. The controversy of their effectiveness in decreasing fossil fuel dependency. Do they make us feel better about our Empire? Are they helping the War on Terror?

How about the mice with human brain cells? The humans with pig tissues? What will we learn about inter-species, genetic modification? How do such amalgams enhance our lives, fighting disease, probing the desire to manipulate life, live a thousand years? Or create cyborgs to do the job? Download intelligence into a computer. O think for me, how much easier that will be . . . What is the matter — the DNA of intelligence — mind/ heart *bodhicitta* — that it could be encased in titanium in plastic in a microchip or dot?

How many more Monsanto abberations? Genetically altered rice that destroys whole cultures? And consummately threatens the food chain.

What is the "great chain of being" these days in a culture that supports the teaching of Creationism? What is a hybridic cosmology? A cosmogony? It seems to be everywhere in anyone's imagination.

What is the tendency to want to time travel, go into 10 directions of space simultaneously?

How about the chimeras of our dreams — part human, part animal? The sadness toward the animal we all feel that comes back to haunt us in manifestations of the atavistic need to kill the things we love, wear them, take on their attributes of name and talismanic power. Eye of hawk, radar of bat. What do we discover about monogamy torquing the genes of the vole?

There's a Burroughsian fantasy of creating a super-being with the advanced attributes of any life form that moves. There's the cut-up and manipulation of organs, transplanting to the best advantage.

Micro-hybrids figure in the most sophisticated technologies, circuits observing MARS, for example, in the project NASA deemed The Structure & Evolution of the Universe Mission.

Or the hybrid technology that supports the X-ray Fluorescence that reveals the Hidden Secrets of Black Holes & Ancient Manuscripts. How many layers can be seen? What is the pentimento? What hand, what hands, what collaborations through time and space?

Pratitya samutpada — Sanskrit for the co-inter-active-interdependency of our existence and beyond — seems to invite a hybrid agenda for empathy and co-existence? Yet falters in the arrogance and prioritizing of the human or the privileged human life style . . .

Hybridity literally refers to the characteristics of plants or animals that are the offspring of individuals belonging to different species.

But this critical theorizing term is widely used now in Postcolonial Theory to describe the newness of many different forms of migrant or minority discourses that flourish in the diasporas of the modern and postmodern periods. Postcolonial Discourse studies the creation of new transcultural forces within the contact zone produced by colonization. Examines, for example, Pidgin English and Creole. Homi Bhabha, one of the main theorists in this field, speaks of the "Third Space of Enunciation," not unlike William Burroughs' "Third Mind," which emerges as a result of collaboration, cannibalizing of text, appropriation, the meeting of two minds etc. Intervention on sacred cows as when Burroughs intercuts lines with Rimbuad, Shakespeare. Ted Berrigan's collaged sonnets also come to mind.

So linguistic cross-breeding as well as imaginal cross-breeding, which might result as a clash of civilizations or cultures or languages or other trajectories of identification. Which could also be a gradual assimilation or exchange.

Thinking of how the United States spreads its ideologies through war and commerce, promoting its stuff, market-driven, etc. And in my own experience of visiting post-World War II Japan, which resists, still, its conqueror; Vietnam where the wounds are still visible, yet you see constantly the hybrids, brought about by American occupation of that country. And thinking of how now, through following the scary "narrative," the "master" narrative, if you will, how much we know — even in our strange myopia — of Islam, of Iraqi "image." It's like using your innocence . . . the incursion and exporting of the west, the rape, the pillage . . .

I've more and more been thinking that poetry is the rival government that can make sense or perhaps more importantly reflect and ponder the strange hybrid mirror. Hélène Cixious has said that the 20th century in its violence has brought about the marriage of Poetry & History, perhaps the most provocative hybrid of all from the standpoint of being writers and artists . . .

Where we must answer with our imaginations to hold the values of the imagination. We need to be not only defenders of freedom but INVENTORS of freedom, as André Breton once advocated (though he kicked Artaud, stupidly, out of the surrealist movement!).

But in a way take on, to continue to take on, new forms. Chinua Achebe has written that

> "New forms must stand ready to be called into being as often as new (threatening) forces appear on the scene. It is like "earthing" an electrical charge to insure communal safety."

Ernesto Cardenal advocates "exteriorismo" — not unlike the strategy of Investigative Poetics where you bring exact data, information, and elements of real life into the work.

Hybrid forms includes performance — words with music, dance, gesture, all manner of transformation.

Hybrid forms include the blurring of distinctions between prose and poetry. Harryette Mullen, Renee Gladman, Bhanu Kapil. Between life and dream. The look is different on the page.

Poetry and essay. Non-narrative prose intervention.

Lisa Robertson's work with architecture. The continuation of projects like Walter Benjamin's *Arcades*, and Gail Scott's *My Paris* which holds a dialogue with *Arcades*.

Inter-textuality — The rhizomic possibilites with computer technology. Word, image, sound, duration . . .

Includes crossing boundaries of many other genres as well. I am working with *sprechstimme* — spoken sung text, with new modal structures, guided by an imagination of VOICE. Forms are embedded within forms in the longer — very much for the page — 800 page so-called Epic. Of gender as well. Who is speaking? Myriad voices of varying disposition. States of mind.

Rage and lullaby. And so on. Going beyond confessional, getting rid of the interference of the individual as ego, as Olson puts it.

As we have discussed, all our work is "political." Is there a conscious hybrid here to engage the political?

The visual — the pictures — photos in the work of — Sebold the novelist, in recent book length texts (Claudia Rankine, just one example), the way Susan Howe draws on marginalia in *Melville's Marginalia*.

Drawing, diagrams, the thrust of documentary visual art to include the word, to parallel the new Orality, Oration.

"When the mode of the music changes, the walls of the city shake," sang Allen Ginsberg.

Body Politic

I invoke the phrase "restored Venus" borrowing from Man Ray's "Restored Venus, 1936" — a gelatin silver print photo of a female replicate torso tied up by ropes — to foreground the irony of the assault on the body.

How to heal up the lone physical body after abuse, after neglect, and by extension the "body politic" when it is also ravaged and dis-membered. When crimes are committed in its name and many bodies are harmed. Guantánamo, Abu Ghraib, all detention centers, all prisons in the US of A and around the world. Dis-remembered. The undisclosed rape of genocidal war. How reclaim the power of compassion when the twisted violence of torture is pandemic? Accountability? To hunt down the perpetrators, stay on the case as many have over half a century with the cold blooded frenzied hate crime of 14 year-old Emmett Till, who as his mother tells it — "had beautiful teeth, they were my pride and joy."

A body is destroyed with malice, with institutionalized neglect, how reclaim its dignity its psyche's imago, its poetics? What is a poetics of body speech and mind in a charnel ground of corpses who rise up once again to say "never again?"

We need witness collectives. We need to "tithe our time," never again, this madness against the body, OUTRIDER citizens, not again, never again. Each individual case. Not the proper care, mis-diagnosis, all-out harm.

We need to investigate and document relevant information and stay on it, go through the courts, work with like-minded compassionate warriors of

Eleni Sikelianos with Anne Waldman, New York City, 2002
PHOTOGRAPH BY LISA JARNOT

Change. Challenge hospitals, prisons. A lifetime of scrutiny and atten-
tion it if need be, and pass that duty on . . . to move all bodies out of
harm's way . . .

      body inflicting harm on another body

           body canonized body revealed

      body *in situ*, in mass grave dug up for forensic analysis

      a tactile art this obfuscation of a *body politics*

pierced by arrow inside the mind

inside the dank isolation cell

fear to look hard, gaze

reclaim: *the act of seeing with one's own eyes*

slammed, shut down, by obvious cover-up

opened not obfuscated by the book

nor obviated
not null & void this research

inquiry

& blasted by daisy cutter we'll record that for all time

a woman's arm gone in the blast

or raped this one, you see? mutilated under hot sun
(sift, sift through the body parts. . .)

not
holocausted body

stop all torture now

domestic & abroad

white phosphorus eating at bodies brought down in Fallujah

body bag body bunker body count body snatcher

corpse cadaver carcass

    this is the political agenda

to fight hypnagogic fascination with death
    with *making* death machines of death

    shift the mind to tender, fearless

      reclamation now

her ability to stand, legs moving walking
    her arms, elbows, hand, lithe fingers stretching
her neck her head her face her ears eyes nose
    throat, speech, speak out. . .

    a poetry.

Rhizomic Poetics

A Conversation (Interview) with Anne Waldman
by Matthew Cooperman

MC: You've recently published *Structure of the World Compared to a Bubble*. It's really an unusual book. It's certainly poetry, but also cosmology; a *doha*, or religiously didactic treatise; a transcription of a pilgrimage; a meditation on walking; a gamelan score; a site map; an "architectural provocation;" an ethnopoetic investigation of nature and culture, the sacred and profane; an "embryonic process into the future;" a peace verse "to check your weapons at the gate," and an ekphrastic narrative which models,
as you point out, "the world as a book." Whew. What was the impetus behind this very complex text? How did you discover the Stupa at Borobudur, and can you talk about the process of writing it, transcribing the stupa literally from Java to Penguin Books in New York?

AW: The first jacket design for the book had the obligatory penguin in his orange nimbus standing surreally in the middle of the cover, which was quite hilarious, since it was hovering over an old stone carving of the Buddha bathing in the Nairanjana River. There were some jokes about the penguin needing to be in a lotus position or in the river with the Buddha but he kept his posture and got moved to the left hand corner.

I had wanted to write a poem for years that examined, investigated, embodied, paralleled through a difficult and resonant language — that might also enfold Sanskrit and Tibetan terms — the remarkable philosophy and psychology of the Bodhisattva path. This is the path of the

Mahayana in Buddhism — and involves a vow to come back lifetime after lifetime to benefit others. There's a narrative, step by step process where you first acknowledge that "suffering exists" and the path unfolds from that hit or *satori*. Another of the Four Noble Truths is the very palpable lesson of impermanence, which we often forget. This inspires you to examine the nature of your own mind. But I was lacking a grid or "structure." And the ideas were abstract, dry and I needed more tangible language and detail. And I was exploring my own understanding of dharma, as a student and sometime practitioner in the formal sense, in other ways. Some essays. Poems like "Makeup On Empty Space," parts of the epic *Iovis*.

But I had been working in Indonesia, specifically with Naropa University's Study Abroad program in Bali since 1988, as a director on several occasions and also running a specific program for writers. And I finally got to take a solo pilgrimage to the famous stupa of Borobudur which sits in the lush and mysterious Kedu Plain, not too far from Yogyakarta, in 1997. This was revelatory, because I was inside a structure that laid out the path most eloquently in its design, architecture, intricate carvings and the physicality of ascent. I started taking notes at the stupa on the spot and spent some days doing the formal circumambulations. The poem became very literally a thinking/walking meditation. That was tracking the experience of the bodhisattva path on many levels.

MC: For such a specific book it also seems very much about contemporary issues of identity and subjectivity, the pitfalls of ego, etc. It feels very necessary and tonic; how "to wake up beyond the identity kit dragged across town and into the forest." Will we ever get over the fascination with the "identity kit?"

AW: It's certainly interesting and I hope salutary. What is the mind really? Where do thoughts come from, where do they go? How are they conditioned by ego? Where does ego fit in? What does it wear? What is its identity? Buddhism suggests you look at a person as a "conglomeration of tendencies" or a hairy bag of water. And of course when you are investigating the meditative mind that's being examined up against what I consider to be the sophisticated psychology of Buddhism you have 2,500 years of history and sutras and practice to contend with. Also a philosophy that profoundly takes on the obstacle of ego.

MC: I'm curious about the reception of the book. I can imagine some of your less buddhistic readers would be bewildered, even put off.

AW: Individual persons have given me encouraging, excited feedback — writers as diverse as Lyn Hejinian, Ron Padgett, Laird Hunt, Thalia Field, Robin Blaser, others — but there have been scant reviews so far (Rachel Levitsky in the *Poetry Project Newsletter* 2005) and I agree there's a level of bewilderment because of the perceived "subject matter." But I had to write this book, it seemed choice-less after the experience of Borobudur. And then became urgent. It was written largely in Italy after 9/11, and pulled together as the war on Iraq was heating up. It became very much a spiritual, almost hermetic practice. Only two pages had been published before publication. But it takes commitment to read it and I hope at least some other poets come to it over the years.

MC: Your performance of the text is also unusual, though not perhaps for you. I've seen you read from it twice now, and the use of gongs and chanting and various "elevations" of speech are very arresting. Could you comment on the performance of *Bubble*?

AW: I think there is an audience for these performances and I am currently developing a DVD called "Tanks Under Trees" (from the "Warring Gods" section) with music by my son Ambrose Bye and footage shot by Ed Bowes (of dancers Douglas Dunn and Grazia della Terza). There's the link to gamelan music, which I've studied, and the notion of "ti bot" — of striking the gong as a way of activating the power and sense of the language. I enjoy playing inside the more performative sections — the dense, prosier "Six Realms" which try to approximate, energetically, the mindset of being animal, of being a war monger as mentioned, or a hungry ghost, or a lotus-land god realm sensualist smoking hashish.

MC: You quote Olson, from the end of "The Kingfishers," in your introduction to the book: "I hunt among stones." As such, *Structure of the World Compared to a Bubble* is also a spiritual biography, an account of such "hunting." Can you talk about how the circumambulation of the Stupa at Borobudur is an apt metaphor for a life and a practice?

AW: As you circumambulate you are studying the stones and what they are depicting — narratives within various sutras, the stories of the Jataka Tales which are the past lives of the Buddha as animals, and so on. And this circling sets up certain rhythms and patterns, which is why gamelan is also the paradigmatic and resonant sound. As a gamelan player you are part of an orchestra of metallaphones and gongs, and you are following your own circular pattern which intersects with another player's circular pattern. Life and its forms are all moving in circles! There's still some mystery concerning the stupa's history. It was most likely completed in 830 C.E. but was abandoned seventy years after its completion. Why? I'm curious. So circumambulating is a metaphor for seeking knowledge and yet in Buddhism you return to where you started, but with new eyes.

"I thought of the E on the stone" is Olson's line also from "The King-fishers." According to Guy Davenport, Olson is referring most likely to the Classical Greek *omphalos* stone which is thought to sit under the pole star. Plutarch conjectures somewhere that the "E" stone at Delphi stands for "ei" or Epsilon which is the second vowel in the alphabet. Also the sun is the second planet, Apollo's planet, and Delphi is Apollo's place. And Delphi is at the center of a circular world, with the stone on one end of the axis and the Pole star on the other. Poets love this kind of hunt. It is a rhizomic practice sending you to encyclopedias, other lexicons, and to travel.

Also I took the Bodhisattva vow — as a pathetic, yet inspired, sentient being — and there's an aspiration to keep the practice of that going. Also the search for the past, in Olson's sense, I think, is also the poets' endeavor. It's arduous and requires poetry making as a guide and re-source. *Istorin:* to find out for oneself.

MC: It seems pretty clear, but what role has travel played in your writing and in your spiritual practice?

AW: A strong role. There's *Structure of the World Compared to a Bubble,* but *Iovis* is also filled with writing that came from investigative travel — India, Nepal, Indonesia, Mexico, South America. I am eager to get back to Asia, especially as the criminal US of A makes its moves in that part of the world. China perceived as the great Enemy requires more mili-tary sites, detention centers and the like. I need to investigate that and also honor the deep layers of those syncretic civilizations — crucibles of fantastic energy, mythology, magic, spiritual power, poetry, dance, gesture. And the natural environments, which are so threatened, endangered. I was last in those environs — in Vietnam in 2000, on the 25th anniversary of the American War, as they call it there — a very powerful occasion, as thousands upon thousands visited Ho Chi Minh's embalmed corpse in a Zen-like mausoleum. This generated "Dark Arcana, Afterimage or Glow," which is a section of *Iovis 3*. This writing began as a journal. It spins around and off the phrase "What is it like to be colonial?"

Surface reality is changing so quickly and we are living in such a scary and "endarkening" time. Thinking of the tsunami and our own shameful Katrina disaster here. The layers of suffering, the extreme poverty, negligence as the planet spins out of control. I've been living vicariously through my son Ambrose of late, who recently visited Angkor Wat. He also went to the killing fields in Cambodia. I guess it's some kind of either genetic or karmic propensity in me — an urgency ensues just contemplating these places — the whole body and mind warms up. I want to be there as some kind of witness.

MC: I've always been impressed by this witnessing aspect, your commitment to an activist poetics. Yet it's also a commitment to poetry as a path. Not surprisingly, this aligns with the Buddhist concept of Refuge. How is the vow to poetry similar to the idea of taking refuge, and is that somehow related to voice, to testimony?

AW: With the Buddhist refuge vow you take refuge in the Buddha, the dharma, the sangha, and you presumably give up personal history and neuroses. You are entering a void of wild mind in a way — no safe reference points, no theism, but the example of the Buddha as a modest, helpful, compassionate person — and there's the truth of reality, of things as they are without manufacturing ownership, and the friendship and support of like-minded folk on this evolutionary spiritual path. And an awareness, also, of the inter-connectedness, the symbiosis of all forms of life. The microcosm is the host for us on this planet. There's a view in radical science that our own human role in evolution is expendable, most fleeting in the context of the rich layer of inter-living beings on the planet Earth's surface. We're guests here and we should behave with dignity and respect. We aren't the rulers of the universe.

And vow is an aspiration, it helps remind you of your original intention to be compassionate. You keep working on it, and you make the gesture to wake up, be less of an egomaniac, with your "body, speech, and mind." So it's the speech part, trying to refine your thinking, your imagination, your aspiration in language, and in poetry. It's also a musical gesture and dance. That's what caught me in the first place, the sounds inherent in language. Down to increments — phones and phonemes that seemed to carry, like a mantra, a certain efficacy, power, magic. But it's fun to play with the high and low guttural sounds, mix them up. I wake myself up this way. I attend to my state of mind with a vocal response to this complicated, illusory world. That somehow your body is a receptacle for mantra which is a part of the "hum."

MC: What is wild mind, wild form? Could you define it in the history and context of an investigative poetics?

AW: There's Gary Snyder's definition of the wild mind being "elegantly self-disciplined, self-regulating." And by extension he says that's what "wilderness" is. Without a management plan. The practice of the wild inspires an "etiquette of freedom." You take care of things because it's beautiful to do so, not out of obligation. I also invoke the rhizome model in Deleuze and Guatari's sense. The Indra's Net of a tuber system, moving horizontally through imagination, space, time and the Buddhist notion of "all 10 directions of space." Awareness is jolted by multiple forces setting additional forces into action. No event is isolated, no force is ever spent. This is wild thinking. It is the basis for a particular poetics that allows for improvisation as well, and the "kinetics of the things." Investigative thinking sets you off to investigating red luminescence under the sea. There's the ecological sense here, the link to other sentient beings and the inter- and co-dependence thereof.

It's a compassionate view, ultimately. And I also use Belgian physicist Ilya Prigogine's term "dissipative structures," which at origin were the first cell-like systems. With an influx of energy, these structures become more instead of less ordered. There's a sense of "autopoietic".— to be alive an entity must actively maintain itself against the mischief of the world. So what do we do with the assault and destruction of Empire?

MC: Your propensity for manifestoes, for declaration, distinguishes your career, and at the same time maintains a central tenet of modernism. Do you see your role in poetry, or one of poetry's at its greatest extension, as necessarily revolutionary? Do you see that quality reviving in the latest generation of poets? How to reconcile modernist proclamation with postmodernism's suspicion of totalizing statements?

AW: The declaiming seems to come naturally. Probably an extension of a sense of Aria, where you need to communicate what's going on in your psyche, in the spotlight. And where the rage is so extreme against the State and its arrogance and deception that it needs to find a comparable heightened form. The times have required strong expressive antics in my own work. One needs to *cut through* discursive mind. This is Diva poetics. Soap Box poetics. You need to shake the walls of the city. You need the "divine terror" Artaud speaks of. These strategies seem universal and timeless and not necessarily locked in an aestheticized sphere or time frame. And the recent Poetry is News events and Poets Against The War activism on the streets of Manhattan and D.C. demand a strain of performance where I might vocalize a strangulation of Donald Rumsfeld — or whoever the demon of the moment might be who seems to have so much control over the lives of others and seems, cruelly, to perpetuate suffering for a pathological ideology — or shriek "I'm in a rogue state" turning into the Rangda witch figure from Balinese ritual theater with trembling fingernails, lolling tongue and sagging tits. I visualize myself on a charnel ground as Durga, Kali, the consummate hag.

It's also the work of Infrastructure Poetics, where one is working and building communities (Many of us have been literally *living* inside community for decades) and feeling the need to represent a larger Voice than my own as an ambassador for poetry and its etiquette and usefulness. It's this irritating messianic thing about how poetry can help save the world. And poetry is the rival government. Revolution is a word that turns many ways, as poet Jack Collom has noted. So the manifestations in the writing and performance are numerous.

And I find the recent writing of Claudia Rankine, Juliana Spahr, Akilah Oliver politically interesting and not either modernist or post-mod. Feminafestos are the preferred mode, but certainly there's an homage there to the polemics of the Surrealists, of Marinetti, Laura Riding. And I've been taken up of late with Syrian-born Arab poet Adonis' excellent "An Introduction to Arab Poetics" which posits — after eloquently guiding the reader through pre-Islamic poetics and concerns, the complication of modernity, and the like — the notion that there is no human dimension in any given period of history without poetry. Poetry is not a stage, but a constituent of human consciousness.

Of course there's the post-modern trope of not wanting to use the language and syntax of the oppressors and decentralizing the confessional "I," and seeing the text as reflexive and more opaque, and interrupting narrative. "Both, both" is the stance on the charnel ground. You trust your sensibility, and you develop your gifts, which you see as *upaya* (skillful means) as everything churns in the maw of the Hag. And you play with it all in the flickering light and shadow.

MC: That's such a sense of performance. You said once, "I think of myself as a speech-singer, a word singer-speaker when I perform" (Joyce Jenkins interview, *Vow to Poetry*) From your World Heavyweight Poetry Championships to your interest in chant and collaboration, you've certainly made performance your touchstone. What are the origins of this style? How much of it is indebted to improvisation and jazz? Or, perhaps conversely, does this speech-singer manifest as a persona, or even a channel? How conscious is it on stage?

AW: The origins go back to childhood performance at home on Macdougal Street (writing, making plays and dressing up) and with the Greenwich House Children's Theater in New York (playing Alice in *Alice in Wonderland,* among other roles). I also worked backstage with the Stratford Connecticut Shakespeare Theater by the time I was sixteen, and there again when I was eighteen with understudy roles and bit parts. Also at Bennington College as Phaedra, and the lead in Lorca's *Blood Wedding.* Lewis Carroll, Shakespeare (I can still hear Morris Carnofsky's Lear in my ear), Greek drama — they can set one on a path.

I was never good at memorization, however, and enjoy being in charge, directing myself and others. I was charged by collaboration, the excitement and urgency of getting ready for performance, the mysterious bifurcation of stage life/real life. But the "style" developed on its own, no models, is not rehearsed. I let the text guide me — how does *it* want to sound? And trust how my body and voice respond as well. Low rumbles, shrieks of rage, operatic *sprechstimme*. I was exposed to a lot of jazz as a child — Steve Lacy was in the extended family — and I trust improvisation within certain frames. The Cage and Stein performances (with others) I've organized over the years reflect a number of strategies. But I trust being on the spot. Poets are very low-tech and prepared for any occasion. I'd like to think there are many personae and yes, assuredly a sense of channeling energy. I usually have a loose plan and the texts might be patched together at the last minute to some kind of random cohesion.

The many pages of *Iovis* lend themselves to intervention and cannibalization. I donned my surgical mask and Vietnamese hat at the last minute at Naropa last summer and was inspired to dance around the room to a tape of my son Ambrose Bye's music with my own voice singing verses of the old Tom O' Bedlam (roots in the 17th century shamanic ballad-poem). This year I wore a black hood à la Abu Ghraib and played another composition by Ambrose to my text, "'Thy' of No Dire Greenhouse Effect," which includes the voice of Eleni Sikelianos and the cries of my infant goddaughter Eva Sikelianos Hunt. I'd been feeling that we live in an insane asylum in this country and wanted that to be the underlying eidolon for these performances.

MC: This is also importantly performance as a female poet. Could you reflect upon your career as such? You've been a lightening rod of female identity in an the at times overwhelmingly male world of poetry. How have you dealt with that? How have the circumstances of women writers changed over the course of your career? What is available now as a feminist project and a poetic?

AW: I'm grateful for all the opportunities I've had in the frequent ways I was able to create zones for poetry, especially through editing, curation of poetry events, directing the Poetry project, co-founding the Kerouac School and so on. Women have to push on claiming infrastructure roles in a range of creative zones. We also don't want poetry to be stuck inside the academy with its master narratives either. There are exceptions, of course, but the struggle continues for equality. Susan Howe, I've heard, was less appreciated and paid less at Buffalo than her male counterparts. Things have changed, however, as we see an unprecedented plethora of publishing of women, terrific small presses like Belladonna, the *Chain* magazine editorship, and women in important teaching roles.

The feminist poetic I see as being a matter of independence — from the constraints of the Language project on the one hand, a facile Beat-trope confessionalism, or identity politics on the other. And a powerful stance that is not so dependent on male forebears or strategies. That has taken off from the *New American Poetry* and been inspired by female forebears Gertrude Stein, Mina Loy, H.D., Lorine Niedecker, Barbara Guest; later contemporaries Susan Howe, Hannah Weiner, Lyn Hejinian, Leslie Scalapino, Norma Cole, Bernadette Mayer, Alice Notley, Kathleen Fraser, Maureen Owen, Eileen Myles, Cecilia Vicuna, Rachel Blau duPlessis. That the shape feels and sounds new, refreshed and has been informed by investigative poetics, performance, race, gender, politics. Not that these are necessary subjects or themes of the work. Translation is important here, as well.

MC: You've mentioned a lot of them, but *as* a feminist poetic, whose work are you most struck with in this regard?

AW: So many activist figures. Sonia Sanchez, June Jordan, the late Audre Lorde, Diane di Prima, the late Muriel Rukeyser. I don't think any of the writing of the poets I am now thinking of could have been written by men. The work of Erika Hunt, Thalia Field, Harryette Mullen, Cole Swenson, Lisa Robertson, Bhanu Kapil, Elizabeth Willis, Eleni Sikelianos, Lisa Jarnot, Elizabeth Robinson, Kristin Prevallet, Akilah Oliver, JoAnn Wasserman, Claudia Rankine, Brenda Coultas, Marcella Durand, others. The litany of all these names through these last questions alone is empowering. And it's engendered a response, an audience, the next wave of strong young women coming up through the ranks. The conversation amongst themselves, and the world through the Internet sustained publication both of poetry and critique has helped. And positions in influential zones — Temple University, Brown, Bard, Naropa.

MC: In a Buddhistic sense, there's a certain paradox in the quest for a "room of one's own." Against impermanence, ambition, desire, a poetry "career" seems, perhaps, overreaching. Or is it? How have you, as a woman, a poet and a Buddhist, accommodated the tensions of this paradox?

AW: Yes, that room is a very different space from the charnel ground. More the necessary alchemical lab, scriptorium, meditation hut. While what I do has the appearance and trappings of "career," I honestly haven't felt it that way in the gut sense. I'm of that Bohemian "tattered bodhisattva" (as Ted Berrigan named it) poet-generation. More of a calling? It chooses you, as Creeley has said. O'Hara, Ginsberg, Olson, Duncan, Dorn, Spicer, James Schuyler, Barbara Guest — invoking their lives and work, the word "career" seems off, inadequate. More like the red-skinned dakini stomping on the corpse of ego, that's the job description.

MC: You talk about this somewhat in your "Feminafesto" as the entrapment of "definition in a heterosexist world," but it's obviously beyond gender. Perhaps I'm essentializing identity, but it's a powerful, and sometimes contradictory, set of impulses.

AW: I think you have to keep in mind the complicated layers of "identity" and how un-solid the overall construct is. The public obligation requires a certain consistency that you, as a poet citizen, can be relied on to serve. Serve the art. Serve the community. I think I felt the "definition in a heterosexist world" to be more of a burden when I was younger. As a younger woman being hit on, or having persons make judgments, assumptions or projections about the expansive poetics and life style I was embracing.

I was identified with Allen Ginsberg, with a strange "crazy wisdom" tantric Buddhist scene. Struggling with simultaneous identities as daughter, lover, wife, mother, teacher, administrator, performer, somehow called on to represent some new wave of woman poet. Struggling with straighter realities trying to fund projects, keep things going, being critiqued, having a strong political activist streak. Trying to have a private life and a public one at the same time. So it's many identities, protean shifts. Not so solid. Sometimes feeling unequal to any task, a failure, a fraud, a jerk, other times confident in the best sense, knowing the right course, taking others along. But ultimately it's the grinning corpse underneath, the charnel ground reality that gives energy. We are here to disappear, is this view. All the more reason to dance, to have a passionate relationship with the world.

MC: We're back to *Structure of the World Compared to a Bubble*, in a sense — your particular path. How does tantric "crazy wisdom" reside in poetic truth and as a poetic life? What can crazy wisdom teach us via poetry?

AW: It teaches something called co-emergent wisdom, which is somewhat like "negative capability" — both, both — living inside and appreciating the paradox or contradiction of reality with "no irritating reach after fact or reason." This co-emergence is alchemical, transformative. And it's a quality Shakespeare has, as Keats says, which is what interests me in poetry and activism. The spiritual view is that every pore in your body is an eyeball and that you are connected to "other" through your vision and breath. You are naturally awake, a seer. But you are lazy, you forget. You are misled by your ignorance, your twisted passion, your aggression. And through practice, training, reminders, flashes of insight, *satori,* you *can* turn your mind around, wake up on the spot, which is also what poetry can help you do. Crack your world, shift your frequency.

So your art, your practice with language is part of that view and is the *upaya* of that view. And you serve it the best you can. But it's fleeting as a construct. It's everything and it's nothing. Breakthrough. To what? Your own impermanence perhaps, the poignancy of your desire, your longing for a more perfect world, your aspiration for love and the love reciprocated, your aching mind which is so vast and curious and powerful and can imagine its own death. Crazy wisdom is heartbreak. Poetry is heartbreak. Something like that.

MC: All of these questions have something to do with witness. Your poetry, and your life *in* poetry, has been a remarkable witness of the times, and an example of how such a witness obtains in a committed practice. Yet the term witness, or more precisely the "poetry of witness," is a highly contested term. Carolyn Forché, in *Against Forgetting*, defines it as that written "out of extremity," political or social. Yet we can witness many things: sexuality, spirituality, gender, the environment, the political landscape, semiotics, social milieu, etc. Is the term as it's used limiting? What does the witness mean to you? Is it useful?

AW: In addition to whatever this simply being AWAKE may call forth in the poetry itself, "witnessing" comes fraught with increased experience, and many years accumulation and a deeper understanding of cause and effect, the way things work. And the need to actually help invent, create situations — communities or schools in my case — or anthologies that attend to the imbalances. So that within the realm of poetry, say, one is going to help other writers be heard. Writers more experimentally inclined. Or writers who specifically take on issues of gender, environment and so on.

And include, always, more women, people of color, cross-gendered writers and so on. One needs to take action out of being witness to injustice, where talented writers are often marginalized. I'm still amazed at how masculinized the fields of critical theory, philosophy, poetics still are, with some notable exceptions.

I've always been interested in the role of the spectator. Where, how, why do we actually engage in what it is we see? What is the provocation toward engagement or action? Of course the artist is always engaged. One is both the spectator and the spectacle as an artist. Or rather, the work is the spectacle. Witness involves being there to testify, as in a trial. But when millions of people watching television see abandoned citizens on rooftops begging for water that doesn't arrive for 4-5 days, what do they do? The challenge is how to see clearly — a racist agenda at work, in addition to the willful incompetence and arrogance of the stewards of our current government. What can one do? One writes a check, participates in hurricane relief benefits, signs on to provide instruments for musicians in New Orleans who lost theirs. It's an endless struggle. And a fragile one. You have to uncover the extremities—of the collateral damage in Iraq, say, because it's not being "shown" to us.

Forché is correct that the work may emerge this way — out of extremity, given the extremity of Auschwitz, Rwanda, 9/11, Katrina, killing fields everywhere — but I don't use the term in my personal poetics. I agree with you. It seems redundant. I assume being/bearing witness is covered in any definition of poetry. Pound's logopoeia, the dance of the intellect (which includes the heart) is always in there.

MC: As another kind of witness, you've seemed to find an unusually fertile wellspring in collaboration. Could you talk about your early experiences of collaboration, say with Lewis Warsh or Ted Berrigan? What has the role of collaboration been in your work, and how has it evolved over the years?

AW: I am currently gathering up the hundreds of pages of collaborations with the help of Daron Mueller for an eventual book, acknowledging the joys of the "third mind," the give and take towards some kind of unified object, or book, or sound. So yes, central to my life in many ways, if you include all the collaboration on projects such as the founding of the Kerouac School with Allen Ginsberg, Poetry Is News project with Ammiel Alcalay and so on. And there are collaborations with artists such as Joe Brainard, George Schneeman, Donna Dennis, Elizabeth Murray, with dancer Douglas Dunn, with musicians such as

Steven Taylor and Bethany Spiers, my son Ambrose, and now video work with Ed Bowes. We made a movie honoring Carl Rakosi for his 100th birthday before he died, based on his poem, "The Menage," and more recently "Colors in the Mechanism of Concealment," which is a response to the torture at Guantánamo.

Ted Berrigan and I worked on "Memorial Day" through the mail, in anticipation of our reading together at St Mark's on Memorial Day in 1974. The date determined the "subject" I collaged together the final version spreading the pages over the floor. We published it as a pamphlet with a cover by Donna Dennis that was handed out at the reading. Lewis Warsh and I primarily worked as editors together, most recently on the *Angel Hair Anthology* (Granary Press 2003), which was based on a magazine and press we started in 1966.

MC: I'm curious about collaboration and gender. Does it tend to manifest as an androgynous poetics? I realize that's a very general question to specific contexts and personalities, but I'm curious if, in your experience, collaboration effaces gender, or more largely questions of identity?

AW: I think the collaboration with painter Elizabeth Murray, "Her Story," has a decidedly playful and energetic ring of the feminine principle. The wit is coming from the women in this series. Her gestures are gorgeous, plastic, comedic. Shapes resembling domestic utensils on a spree, kinetically expand the language. Eileen Myles and I worked on a collaboration entitled "Polar Ode" which has an erotic subtext toward one another that's not heterosexual. The work on stage is usually dominated by my voice and lyrics. I've recently been working with the mandolin playing of poet Bethany Spiers who has herself an androgynous sound. Very delicate, and then fierce at times. But in working with oth-

ers gender is not the primary modus. And I would say that the out-
comes of a number of different kinds of collaborations are various,
polyvalent.

MC: Given that you were interviewed, you've obviously seen Daniel
Kane's book *All Poets Welcome: The Lower East Side Poetry Scene in the
1960s.* He suggests a fundamental shift toward the communal in Ameri-
can poetry during that tumultuous time, at least as exhibited by the
scene at Les Deux Magot, Le Metro, and later the St. Mark's Poetry
Project. Would you agree that "all poets were welcome," or that the fa-
milial ethos of that time marked a real shift in not only acceptance, but
collective practices and procedures?

AW: I would say, generally, yes, all poets were welcome. Not "all poets"
were drawn to the exigencies of the Lower East Side scene, however. We
took matters into our own hands, created alternatives to the uptown lit-
erary mafias, and essentially created our own "little universe," our own
economics of publishing and so on. We empowered ourselves. Yes, it
certainly changed things, it radicalized the sense of "scene" of commu-
nity. We had a base of operation, also, to protest the war in Vietnam, to
work side by side with other communities such as the Young Lords, the
Theater Genesis folk, the filmmakers. There were precedents surely, but
having that particular site — of St. Mark's, which continues now after
forty years with "lineage holder" Anselm Berrigan currently at the helm
— made a tremendous difference.

MC: Kane's book really emphasizes and details the material practices of
the poets of the East Village — how mimeo magazines, and the resulting
underground status many of the rags had, developed the quickening of
an alternative poetics. So too, it might be the obscenity trials of Grove

Press, or *Yugen*, or *Fuck You: A Magazine of the Arts*. Was there a sense of collective resistance? And was that similar to the inception of the slightly later *The World*?

AW: Yes, there was a sense of collective enterprise. The "alternative poetics" had to do with economics, with urgency, with getting work-in-progress out as it was written. Which then would engender a response and perhaps guide the way the writing would go. It enhanced the conversation *as writers*. We were developing as writers. Why wait around to get published by an uptown publisher? There's an isolation in that process, constant hope and fear. We would also work collaboratively late at night, invite the community to "collation parties." Do these one-shot items for occasions like birthdays, marriages. There's a wonderful collection of those in my archive at The Hatcher Graduate Library in Ann Arbor.

A lot of other poets were also using the mimeo presses — *Telephone, Adventures In Poetry, Angel Hair, Dodgems*. I remember Joel Oppenheimer's wife Helen reading my palm once forty years ago and saying (she was joking no doubt), "You will always be loyal to the poetry underground," and although I publish some of my work with Penguin, I still do small press editions with Erudite Fangs, a modest random imprint.

MC: The scene at St. Mark's in the mid to late 60s was an extraordinary artistic florescence — Theater Genesis and Sam Shepard, the Rev. Michael Allen's Vietnam protests, the Millennium Film Project, the publication of *The World*, but also, as you've mentioned, *Adventures in Poetry, Angel Hair, Lines, O to 9, Caterpillar*, etc., various jazz concerts. All that free love and hippie rebellion . . . what a remarkable time and place! Could you talk about that moment, that flowering of creativity as a model for artistic rebellion? I mean, we live in such a cynical age now, and it seems hard to imagine such momentum.

AW: "First thought best thought." Not so beholding to self-censorship or fear of being exposed, embarrassed because of one's naiveté or lack of the proper education and pedigree. The elitist barriers were down. Some kind of wonderful candor, openness, compassion, tolerance. In hindsight I have to see the "flowering" as a spiritual movement that had art and poetry and so many other kinds of manifestations as its *upaya*. It wasn't caught up with the academies, institutions and their karma, which rests so heavily on investments that usually feed on the suffering of others.

There was a kind of invention and intervention going on you don't see enough of these days. And bravado. People were not afraid to go to jail, or resist paying taxes. Not to say that interesting writing or thinking isn't happening now, but it's so contained within comparatively safe zones. Although I really see that as an illusion, ultimately. With censorship on the rise and the right-wing Campus Watch on the move targeting activist writers, who knows?

I mean back then, there was so much less inhibition, less coding going on. There was an exuberance of language and experience that could be explored, and because we were "below the radar" there was the sense of operating out of an alchemical laboratory. There was also a growing democratization of the sexes, less old-boy than the Beats, say, or Black Mountain. It was the work also of O'Hara, Ginsberg, Diane di Prima, McClure, John Wieners and others. We had them as precedents.

MC: What can we do to foster such "openings" now?

AW: The Naropa Summer Writing Program attempts to continue some of that spirit of candor and mutual support, and often I wish it could all be free. Some of us have even talked about a "free university." Tithe our time toward collective projects. All writers should engage in some kind of small press publishing at least once in their lives. Or help create a gallery or center in a small storefront in Denver or Detroit or Boston, wherever you happen to be. And keep the doors open. It might be important to organize even more politically. Boycotts, start hugging the trees again, etc. There are still some useful strategies from the old days. And folk in schools should continue to organize conferences but break down some of the structures of that paradigm. I'm training to work in radio.

MC: Radio? Air Waldman? Can you tell me more about this?

AW: Radio as a rhizome of possibility, as a way to take back the voice from pop mainstream iconic culture, talking heads, from the passing dumbed-down TV show. And I know when I listen to intelligent radio I feel more engaged. You think more without the pictures, or you create the pictures. As you would in reading poetry. There's room for the imagination. Of course both radio and television are means to something more utopic, alternative.

MC: Did you know Paul Blackburn well? He seems like such a seminal figure in the Lower East Side Poetry scene, particularly as a literary organizer. I think he's dramatically undervalued as a poet. His *Journal* poems, to me, are a magnificent achievement, and his early death from cancer really a tragedy. I wonder why he's not more highly considered.

AW: He was modest, died too young, needs an energetic literary biographer. There is so much more to investigate from this period, in these individuals — their work, their thinking across language, culture, history. It's key to an understanding of the time, of the the world, understanding the "human" before it's too late. I more and more insist that one must go to the poets for the real history. I knew Paul, visited his home on many occasions. He was studious, sympathetic. I admire his troubadour translations collected in *Proensa*, his own ramble, his own writing so like those he loved. I would walk with him from 7th Street hauling the heavy Wollensack to record the readings at St. Mark's. He saw the value of the tape archive and taught me that incalculable value from the start, which is why we record everything so assiduously on tape and then digitalize it at Naropa.

MC: Ted Berrigan was a close friend, and fellow collaborator. He appears again and again in the annals of the times as a truly catalyzing figure? What made him so special?

AW: His generosity, his ability to make you feel inspired to great heights of genius and knowledge. He took Olson's *istorin* — to find out for oneself — literally to heart. It was as if someone told you that you know everything you need to know, that you can just "go on your nerve" (O'Hara) and you will have a rich and full and wonderful life forever. His line "I am in love with poetry/this my weakness smites me" says a great deal about him actually. He was bear-like, dominating, irritatingly bossy even, but made delicate by his passion for poetry. He was perpetually "smitten." He loved people, was immensely curious. Time with him was rich and exciting. He walked around scrutinizing the phenomenal world with humor and amusement. I loved going to galleries with him, dropping in on painters. His huge *Collected Poems,* recently published by University of California Press, is a testament to his tremendous generosity as a poet. His radical *The Sonnets* are unsurpassed poems in that "form."

MC: Could you tell me a little about the early stages of the Poetry Project? Blackburn's getting passed over for Joel Oppenheimer, and the fallout from that, seems to have riven the community. And yet that was also the beginning of your "official" relationship. If I'm not mistaken, you were the Assistant Director under Oppenheimer? And then, after the brouhaha, became Director?

AW: That's documented in Kane's book fairly accurately. Yes, there was a rift as Paul was the one who had been running the open readings at the Church the year before (and at Le Metro Café before that) and had more "entitlement" to the job. Joel had been working as a printer and was less a community organizer. I wasn't privy to this earlier history in that I hadn't been on the premises. I felt I had to proceed with the job as defined, but then clearly Joel wasn't that interested in being an administrator and it fell more and more to me. But I always respected Paul and wondered how he might have fared with the administrative work himself. In hindsight, it needed to be carried by the younger generation. There were some rifts already in that older generation. I was only twenty-one when I started working there.

MC: You held that position for a decade. How did the Project develop under your tutelage, and how did that translate into the kind of community you envisioned at Naropa?

AW: Suffice it to say, I wanted to transplant some of that structure and energy to Naropa and think I was able to do that over the years, luring many of the writers from that community to guest residencies and the like. The difference of course is the town of Boulder vs. the Lower East Side. But we also had to build and create community in Boulder, just as we did in New York City.

MC: *Fast Speaking Woman* is such an important text in your oeuvre. As an articulation of second-wave Feminism, it unleashed a very real force in American poetry and, as such, a permission. And yet, as Maria Damon has pointed out, it escapes an essentializing of gender through the dimension of chant. In this regard it brings in a whole shamanistic practice into poetry. You take that, as you say, from the Mazateca Maria Sabina. As a kind of ethnopoetic translation, it pushes American poetry into uncharted atavistic memory, on the one hand, and the whole tradition of oral poetries from Homer to the Celts to Native Americans and Tibetan chant. It's also a radically destabilizing text as a resistance to power, whether that be the poetry establishment or the military-industrial complex in this country. Could you discuss that poem (and book) as a seminal phase of your career, and how that led, in certain ways, to *Iovis*?

AW: I've discussed this a bit in an essay entitled "Fast Speaking Woman and The Dakini Principle" (this is also in Rothenberg/Joris's *María Sabina: Selections* [University of California]) where the notion of the dakini — or female sky walker, protean shape-shifter in Tibetan mythology — takes hold as a kind of ur-energy, traveling through language with assertion, commanding herself into being. And the text is indebted to Maria Sabina, one of the great oral poets of the last century, a woman without formal education, barefoot much of her life. It was seminal because it gave permission to sustain the voice in a public sphere and in a contemporary sphere. And the edition which included other 'chants' seemed a cultural intervention at the time. The 20th anniversary edition included more poetics, and particularly the essay "I Is Another: Dissipative Structures," based on a talk given at Naropa which lays out a personal poetics of performance. Allen Ginsberg and Kenneth Koch were both "taken" by this work, they heard it in the early 1970s as a breakthrough and further encouraged me to "write long." Kenneth appreciated the vibrato which pleased me since there's clearly this operatic thrust in my physiognomy and imagination. This appears more pronouncedly in sections of *Iovis*, particularly the "Pieces Of An Hour" (for John Cage), and the *sprechstimme* of "Devil's Working Overtime."

I wanted to create an epic that would be a life's work which would be multi-faceted in its language, forms, themes, and would sing myself both into being and dissolving, and that would have a more cyclical structure, less narrative, linear, and that would inspire survival of the most ancient and fundamental "consciousness" of poetry. For myself and others. And there's that quality of outlasting the machine, the war machine. Epic has interested me from the start of my poetic yearnings. It is the ultimate dissipative structure and autopoiesis.

MC: *Iovis* can be placed alongside the great long poems of the 20th century — the *Cantos; Paterson; "A"; The Maximus Poems; The Dream Songs; Gunslinger; Ark;* etc. Yet those all stand variously as emblems of a phallocentric language. Could you talk about *Iovis* as both a practice of lineage and a practice of gender? You invoke an essential maleness — literally, "all is full of Jove, or sperm" — and yet the poem's clearly a feminist revisioning of the lineage, and a questioning of male "mastery." It's similar to *Fast Speaking Woman* insofar as it deconstructs boundaries of gender and identity, yet it clearly wants a conversation with the epic tradition. That's a delicate tightrope.

AW: I think it sustains that conversation and is part of the lineage and also reclaims epic for a female imagination with new priorities. I sing of war, but not of its glory. I sing down war. I list all I know of war and invert it, transmute it in my song. I include the voice of the male child that doesn't seek out war. I honor the hermaphroditic imagination. I honor and investigate the time I am born in as a seer. I include detritus, details, mythologies, science, Buddhism, stories of others, heartbreak, *fellaheen* worlds, and respect for the gnosis of the past and the future. I want to hold the mirror up to the Patriarch.

MC: *Iovis'* technique is also a kind of revisioning of tradition. There isn't a master narrative of quest, conquest or journey underlying it, nor is it a graph of maturation, nor a study of place. One might argue that, in its informality and inclusivity, it's a journal, a journal poetics. Or one might say that, through its lack of a mastering "center," it enables a new kind of chromosonal hybridity, what you've earlier described as a rhizomic model. Yet it's also dramatically intertextual, intercultural. It's really like nothing else around. Could you talk about the structure and technique of *Iovis*? What drives its scale and scope and method? How did that evolve over three books and a decade of composition?

AW: It began in the mid-80's — this is 20 years now. I had traveled back to India. And there was also an important trip to Nicaragua. How could I make links between these disparate travels (and some of that writing remains to be included in the poem), between my Colorado life, based in sustaining the Kerouac School project, and my New York life. Also being a relatively new mother (Ambrose was born in 1980) I was having ideas and visions about the terrifying world from the point of view of this pulsing, palpable, very new life in my arms. And the queries and speech of the child. And the sense of interruption that occurs all the time. Ambrose in a way was the Muse for *Iovis*, and continues to be. "Mom, you are so random" is one of his refrains. I needed to make sense of the world for his sake.

It was a beautiful task I set upon, an act of love. I wanted to capture the metabolism of my own thought-patterns relative toward "other." And I wanted to be intelligent about other and get inside or question *its* metabolism.

I am actually very turned on and distracted much of the time by just about anything I read, see, investigate, and where I travel to. What form could hold all this? Homages to Sappho, King Lear, H.D. and Kerouac? The canto is ideal, and the exigeses, précis could work, and there needed to be room for dreams and luminous details. But you'll notice Book I is more male centered, Book II moves out to the female, and androgynous. "3" (as I'm calling it) is so caught up with the current version of being under assault, that gender becomes confused. There was an original plan of 24 sections or chapters within each book — the hours of a day. There are also recurring motifs, phrases. "Anne grasping the broom more tightly now." I am driven still by unworldly love, which was Dante's muse.

MC: Can you tell me a little bit about the Michigan conference "Makeup on Empty Space: A Celebration of Anne Waldman"? How did that conference come about, and why did you decide to locate your papers at the University of Michigan. In terms of institutional affiliation, that seems like a slightly odd location.

AW: The wonderful, astute librarians at the Hatcher Graduate Library were interested in starting a "rebel poets" holdings. They also wanted a living poet who would continue to generate energetic text and projects. And the range and evidence of activism, Buddhism, founding schools, editing magazines, was voluminous, in addition to the manuscripts, correspondence, tapes, photos, other documents. Bill Morgan, one of Allen Ginsberg's archivists, was instrumental in the arrangements. And it was very timely as there had been a water pipe burst at my home on Macdougal Street in New York, where some of the archive was stored, and other boxes were gathering dust and pigeon droppings in a barn in Cherry Valley.

I also needed the financial support for new projects. The University of Michigan had one of the first sit-ins during the Vietnam war. It's always been a liberal, if not radical place. I visited the White Panthers back then, and also was there with Allen and John Lennon and Yoko Ono for the John Sinclair benefit. I was almost a Hopwood scholar there, I evidently came in second when Gregory Orr got the position. I used to visit Donald Hall there, at the university. Frank O'Hara had been a student, Ted Berrigan taught there in the 70s. The Alternative Press harks from Michigan. There's some context and history. I've been meditating a lot on then notion of "Archive" as we continue to struggle to preserve the Naropa holdings. My archive is really about "others" as much as it is about me. It's a symbiotic display.

MC: I'd like to return to *Vow to Poetry* to end. In the interview with Randy Roark you say, "I took a vow early on to never give up on poetry or on the poetic community — to serve as a votary to this high and rebellious art." The vow here is to poetry, but as Maria Damon points out in her *Jacket* essay, "Making the World Safe for Poetry," it is also a vow *through* poetry. That is, the end and the means, the goal and the vehicle are conflated, though they are not necessarily the same thing.

Could you address this interesting tension, both in your work, and in the larger sense of commitment our times seem to call for. The war in Iraq, surveillance at home, hurricanes, bird flu, religious polarization. . . we live in such troubling times. What can we do to "keep the world safe for (and through) poetry?"

AW: Yes, I would agree it's a vow *through* poetry at this point. That is perhaps the skillful means, poetry as access to understanding — gnosis — what have you — which of course inevitably leads to more curiosity, more investigation. I want to go back to the Prephanerozoic Era! Or consider the lifespan of slime molds down the great chain of being. From the point of view of life on this planet, humans have only just arrived. We can't trace back more than a few thousand years before the past is murky, and we are still, now, learning to be human. We're close to our microbial forebears and we could learn something from them about survival, about co-existing, about inter-connectedness — *pratitya-samutpada* — about the mutual interlocking "dance" of existence and a longer view.

I think sometimes that poets are best prepared for the current troubles because they have no expectations of worldly gain, because they have an ear on the ancient lineaments and music of the past, have experienced heartbreak in great lines of poetry and "history," are curious and open about the future, and are more willing to work together now — more so perhaps than other communities. And enraged too at the ignorance and arrogance of plutocracy which holds power and induces relentless suffering. But willing, as poets, with nothing to lose to "speak to power." This is only *a version of the world*, remember. But we must stop the killing of war. It's a tired obsolete model, humans can do better than this. It's not necessary to survival. And we need to be better stewards and guests of this planet and take care of one another and the other denizens: everyone should have food and clothing and education and health care. And justice and freedom.

Noting and participating in the Women In Black vigils, I thought of Herakleitos out of which a whole section of *Iovis* 3 emerged ("Worrying Your Logos: Conversant You Speak To the Dead"). It was the ritual for war dead combined with the aphoristic and ironic logic of the philosopher that entered my mind. "The hidden attunement is better than the obvious one," or "if there were no sun there would be night," and so on.

And then the Buddhist aphorism "be a child of illusion" crept in, which has to do with feeling *inspired* by the ephemeral quality of existence. The opposite of delusion. And the drug referred to in these lines represents the darker pull or side of the samsaric world. Although it too wakes up to "the present." That everything can be such an illusion and so beautifully transient is the very reason you fight for this "existence" and stand by your word:

> . . . *later that same night not quite dozing the pill having worn thin it occurred to me that in an attempt to control the future according to our fates (woman's character is her fate) we live a Devil's variance with Heraclitus' time zone. We exist in a false construct where we can appreciate the contrivance.*

The drug spoke to me and said
there would be no time like the present

[Be a child of illusion]

it rests by changing

¡No pasarán!

---

line drawn in the sand

FROM: *Iovis 3: Colors in the Mechanism of Concealment*

Anne Waldman, "Music and Poetry for Progressives," Boulder Theater, 2006
PHOTOGRAPH BY HR HEGNAUER

"Thy" of No Dire Greenhouse Effect

Yea tho I am walking
yea tho I walk forever in thy direction which is thy "thyness"
yea tho thy "thyness" be friendly
that it be no shadow, that it be no death
yea that thy "thy" be willing, be aura, be oracular
yea that "thyness" be without gender without godhead
godhead is no way to be walking towards "thy"
thy is no kingdom come
thy is no purple privileged glory
thy is no flag, no rod, no scepter, no staff of brutality
thy is no random particle
thy is a kind site of no dire greenhouse effect
thy is a place with conscientious war tribunals
thy is of mercy and follows all the days of tracking war criminals
thy is the hours of constant tracking
thy will keep you awake in any time zone tracking
because thy is observation, is a current affair, is tracking "thy"
thy goes back to any older time you mention
a time the increments of language were simpler, were strange
thy was a module, thy was a repository
thy was a canticle for future discipleship
thy is architecture, thy is the entire book for the things of "thy"
thy is a book of thy "thyness" which is not owned
can you guess the "thy" in all the days of my defiance?
yea tho I fear thy terror of "thy" amnesia, thy negligence

yea tho it stalks me in the valley
yea that it beseeches me to lighten up
yea tho it behooves me to abdicate "thy"
I will keep the sleep of ancient times
    of Arcady of the holy cities where thy hides
thy could be done, thy could be stationary in any language
    and then thy could be moving as I do in pursuit of sanity
that they track the war profiteers
that they track the war criminals
that they track the murderers
    who slaughter innocents
that they are exposed in the market place
that they are brought to justice.

Revolution / Evolution

AN INTERVIEW WITH ERNESTO CARDENAL
by Anne Waldman

I had the good fortune of being in residence in the fall of 2001 at the Civitelli Ranieri Center in Umbria, Italy, with Ernesto Cardenal — major poet (author of *Cosmic Canticles*), Catholic liberation theology priest, and former Minister of Culture under the Sandinistas. Ernesto is one-of-a- kind — a citizen of the world, an international treasure. We were both "fellows" on writing retreats, right after the terrorist attacks in the US and as the bombing began in Afghanistan. Ernesto was well into the fourth book of his memoirs focusing on the Nicaraguan Revolution. I was concentrating on a series of manifestos on current events and a long poem based on research in Indonesia. We would greet each other in the morning, exchange political email news, see if the *Herald Tribune* had arrived, converse in broken Spanish and English and take side trips with our comrade fellows (from Ghana, Trinidad, Mexico, and Australia). It was a very intense (and tense) time to be together. One heartening event was the Peace March from Perugia to Assisi (right after the bombing began) with 200,000 concerned citizens in attendance — priests, children, the Women In Black, Palestinian refugees, Greenpeace activists. It gave some energy and opposition to what we perceived as a kind of denial on the US landscape — that in spite of the horrific events of September 11, every human life is precious and war on innocent civilians is not a solution for World Peace.

Anne Waldman: I would like to ask you first, Ernesto, at what point poetry seemed most relevant to, and connected with the struggles of the Sandinistas and their supporters. Was it in the beginning of the Revolution, during the period of creating a new society and in your role as Minister of Culture? Did poetry help and have a role in the struggle with the Contras?

Ernesto Cardenal: The most important poetry in Nicaragua had been before the Revolution. The great poets of the country were during Somoza's time. Although all were Somoza's opposers, some were jailed, others were exiled, others died while fighting. From Ruben Dario up to the present, we can say poetry was revolutionary and prepared the ground for the Revolution. It created a conscience in the people. Not that everyone read poetry, they were just a few, but poetry influenced people who influenced others who didn't read poetry, and prepared them for the Revolution. And, in turn, the Revolution influenced the poetry that came after it too. It wasn't just poets who influenced the Revolution, but also novelists, painters, musicians, writers of protest songs. Poetry was very useful for the Revolution, together with painting, theater, music as well as the Poesía Popular that was created by the poetry workshops of the Ministry of Culture. There was poetry from the barrios, workers, campesinos, and also from the armed forces, the army, and the police. In the battle with the Contras, there were always poets, mostly young poets fighting in the armed forces, as well as artists and painters.

AW: I know that you were a friend to Allen Ginsberg. Like you, Allen was in many ways a statesman and a political activist. In these trying times we seem to have fewer public poets, fewer international ambassadors who are able to articulate sanity with an inspired tongue, an inspired language. Would you comment on your friendship with Allen? And the loss of his presence in the cultural-political arena?

Anne Waldman and Ernesto Cardenal with artists Mario Lewis and El Anatsui,
Civitella Ranieri Center, Italy, 2001
PHOTOGRAPH BY CLAUDIA CANNIZZARO

EC: I am glad to have known Allen Ginsberg. We were studying at Co-
lumbia University in New York at the same time, although we never met
there. Later we met, and we found out we had attended the same univer-
sity. Columbia was very big — at that time something like 40,000 stu-
dents (in attendance). Many years later we met in New York City and
other places. Then he came to Nicaragua. He came twice. The first time
he visited with a big group of North American writers. The Russian poet
Yevtushenko was there at the same time. We made a declaration, the three
of us — Ginsberg, Yevetushenko, and myself — on the things we agreed
upon, and then on other things which we denounced. Both of them also
attended an important cultural event — the Poetry Marathon that took
place every year in the city where Rubén Darío was born. People would
listen to poetry for eight or nine hours at a time. The best poets of Nica-
ragua and the poets from the poetry workshops were there, as well as

some of the commandantes of the Revolution (Tomas Borge, Daniel Ortega, Sergio Ramirez).

Ginsberg and Yevtushenko admired the marathon very much. Yevtushenko said that in the USSR he'd never seen people mixing with the police and the military forces so much, and reading poetry together. Ginsberg gave important support to the Revolution when he visited. I believe he was the best US poet of his generation. A very distinctive poet for his prophetic power, for his social and political denunciations. Because of these things he was one of those poets who, in Ezra Pound's term, might be called an "antenna of the race." It is a shame that you don't have a public figure like Allen now in contemporary poetry, who goes out to the people as he did, as you said. It is a big loss.

AW: You mentioned to me that you thought Fidel Castro's act of expressing condolences to the US after the September 11 attacks in New York and Washington, D.C. as one of bravery and dignity. Would you care to comment further? And how do you see the future of Cuba in the world? Of course Cuba is still an inspiration for so many people, in spite of the controversies and difficulties within. The fact that Cuba has stood up to the US giant for so long. Many artists who travel there come back moved and inspired. So if you would comment on the situation there and how you see the future.

EC: Castro's condolences for the terrorist attacks against the US seem to me a very noble gesture since his country has been a victim of Cuban terrorists who have been supported by the US for many years. He has also, personally, been the victim of many assassination attempts by the CIA. The most important thing to remember about Cuba is that it is the only country in the world that doesn't submit to the US, that rebels against US hegemony and is actually the only socialist country at the moment in the world. Talking about the lack of basic things such as food, health and education. Certainly Cuba has great economic problems, but this is due in large part to the forty year-long embargo that the US has imposed on it. The embargo has distorted the economy, as well as created inequalities, in spite of it being a socialist country. The embargo also has created bad things such as prostitution, which at least is different from other countries because the basic needs of the women are covered. The prostitution is not motivated by economic need, but by consumerism.

One of the most important results of the Cuban Revolution is that endemic diseases that are still found in other Latin American and third world countries have been eradicated in Cuba. That suggests a better standard of living. It means better conditions in hygiene, housing, potable water, etc. It is not enough to eradicate disease. You've got to eradicate the other conditions of poverty. In addition, Cuba has always had great results in the field of sports, getting more medals than other countries who are very much wealthier and developed than Cuba. This achievement in sports has taken place even though it is such a small country, with three million inhabitants, and with the difficulties of the embargo. It is a lot of work for a country to have sports champions. For example, to cultivate a champion swimmer, you need to start training eight year-old children who will require special food and other training conditions to maintain a competitive edge to be a world champion. Cuba's ability to win medals suggests a total transformation of the population. I will finish by saying that a few days ago a friend of mine from Santa Cruz, California, went to Cuba. He was surprised to see so much happiness and joy in the people. He's a psychologist, and just by seeing people's faces, he could tell they were happy.

AW: You have been working on Volume 4 of your memoirs which focuses on the period and history of the Revolution in your country. Rather than a memoir of the past, do you see this documentation as being both helpful and hopeful for readers, writers, activists coming later?

EC: Yes, because it's been a very beautiful Revolution. The most important event in Nicaragua's history. A Revolution with a great heroism, generosity, comradery, that awoke the solidarity and affection of the whole world. Because we all are forgetting this period in Nicaragua, and in the rest of the world, because the Revolution has been slandered — that is why I am working on my memoir. Especially to let the younger people know, to prepare them for a new revolution. We are waiting for it, though we haven't seen any signs of it yet. Before Somoza's time too, we waited for the Revolution for a long time. And we announced the revolution even though there wasn't any sign of it.

AW: In conversation you mentioned that the "hope of the future" for revolution would be in the next generation who are mere children now. That as the world grows speedier, more consumerist, more globalized, more threatened environmentally than ever before, more armed for advanced warfare and surveillance — as we are seeing now in the war on terrorism and the bombing of Afghanistan, and further down the line the weaponization of space, genetic manipulation and so on — it is hard to imagine a change of heart, which is really what I see and I'm sure you see is needed — a spiritual and truly compassionate paradigm shift. Could you say more about what your view of the future would be? How can one be optimistic in the face of such oppressive forces and also a world that seems once more on the brink of a larger war?

EC: Revolutions, social changes are coming. Years ago in the US, a protest by young people against the Vietnam War was initiated by two people: a Vietnamese man and a North American woman. I was brought

to visit this woman in New York. She was rich and she invited me to din-
ner. I went there during the Nicaragua Struggle for Liberation to ask her
to do for us the same thing she had done during the Vietnam War. She
said that was impossible because at that time, American youth, in and out
of the universities, were apathetic, uninterested in anything social or po-
litical. An apolitical generation, she said. Not as before, when they had
started the protest against the Vietnam War. But she said that this condi-
tion was going to change again.

It indeed changed: in Nicaragua and in the rest of the world. Even though
now we have another apathetic apolitical, disillusioned generation. It
doesn't trust any political parties, nor its leaders. It's consumerist, interested
in entertainment only, and in its own wealth and individual life. But, I've
seen that the youngest, the teenagers, and even children ten years old, have
grown interested in politics, in social revolution, and not just in Nicaragua,
but also in other parts of the world. Not long ago I met with Yevtushenko
in a congress with writers in Chile. He told me the same was happening
in Russia. We can tell that the new revolution will be different, without
leaders, without political parties. Surely it will not be violent, as the last
one of the 20th century, and the first of this century — the one of the
Zapatistas and Sub-Commandante Marcos in Chiapas, that doesn't have
any political party nor aspire to the presidency of the country or political
power. I believe that we'll see other revolutions, because of the laws of
evolution. Evolution moves along with the history of humanity, making
our species more united, humans more entwined, with advances in com-
munication, with ever higher velocity and intensity.

The Jesuit evolutionist Pierre Teilhard de Chardin, a paleontologist and
mystic, said during World War II that movements such as Nazism and fas-
cism were crises of growth. Communication's intensity produces a tighter

unity within people, and more conflict among people. The horrifying attacks on the United States from the other side of the world are indicative of the intensity of current mass media which in turn can create what Teilhard refers to as crises in growth.

AW: I was struck by the thinking and prescience of some of the lines in your "Cantiga 8" (from *Cosmic Canticle*), your epic poem of extraordinary magnitude and beauty, as well as philosophical, cultural, scientific, historical, political astuteness, in light of the recent attacks on the World Trade Center in New York:

> Sunday night on Wall Street and a foul wind
> Blows newspapers along the empty sidewalk. Wall Street
> With stars eerie and empty. The bank windows dark
> Though not all. A few rows lit up
> In the black monstrosities. They can be identified:
> The foreign departments of the big banks
> The iron doors barred & padlocked.
> But by back doors some people have entered
> The foreign departments. The lights — secret meetings,
> decisions we're unaware of (and the cigar smoke
> rising like shares) but they affect us all.
> Devaluation sparks off a riot in Malaysia, buses burned
> And blood flows in the streets like water from a hydrant
> At the hour that the stars shine over Wall Street
> And the hour the banks open in London.

Obviously intelligent and progressive thinking articulates the horror of US capitalism and hegemony in the world but poetry seems to cut to the quick of the matter. And you also say in this Canticle that capitalism will pass away. Your poetry harbors insight, wisdom, and prophecy, and perhaps all the answers to any question I might ask would be in this epic poem. Poetry is often prophetic. Do you see the recent terrorist attacks, obviously carried out with great "method in their madness," as inevitable?

EC: I wrote another poem titled "Journey to New York," where I mention the two towers. I speak about the twin towers being taller than the Empire State Building and that it was Sunday night, and they were illuminated from the middle to the top. And I said that the exploitation going on in the world was coming from these towers. I said that the banks were screwing up half of humanity. These attacks against the United States were against capitalism and imperialism. The symbols are Wall Street and the Pentagon. This doesn't justify the attacks. It was utter madness as you say. But the Pentagon and Wall Street aren't innocent either. A fruitful outcome would be the conversion of the system, but we don't see that yet. Bush said the attacks were against freedom and democracy, but we see that they really were attacks against capitalism and imperialism. Bush also said it's the struggle of good against evil. In reality it is evil against evil. Evil creates another evil, and in between there are so many innocent people caught in the middle, east and west. I hope in the future many more people in the US will understand that they live in a bad system and that they have to change it.

AW: The complications and karma of current terrorist attacks and the world response and all the international backdoor deals seem too much for one mind to grasp. How do we know what is real when there is such a "manufacturing of consent" in Noam Chomsky's phrase? What can we trust?

EC: Let me tell you that I never heard of Osama bin Laden before September 11. I could not spell his name. Why? Because he wasn't mentioned in the media. I suppose that there are many like me who would say the same. Now we all know him. All we get is media from the United States that both informs and misinforms us, just like in totalitarian countries where you don't have any intermediary information of any sort. The US never mentioned bin Laden, since he was a CIA creation. And he was with the Contras during the Nicaraguan Revolution, as we learned from the Iran-Contra scandal. The CIA also organized Afghanistan against the USSR. The Taliban, another CIA creation, wasn't mentioned very much either. Until now. Now we all know about it because it turned out to be an enemy. It is clear that they are playing with our heads. Currently, the one million victims in Iraq are still unknown in the US. The truth can only be fathomed from independent sources. Noam Chomsky is one of those sources for me. We have to find a way to receive alternative information.

AW: As a radical Catholic priest who has practiced "liberation theology" and was stripped of religious authority and "declared an outlaw," could you say something please about how your faith sustains you in these times?

EC: I believe capitalism will end because it is an unjust system, and because the laws of evolution are about more and more union, more and more love among our species. Particles unite to form the atom, atoms unite to form the molecule, molecules unite to form the organism, organisms unite to form the society. And society, for some time now, tries to have less and less inequality. We overcame slavery and feudalism, and now it's time to overcome capitalism. Later on we'll surpass socialism too. Then we'll have a perfect system. Then we will be in the Kingdom of Heaven.

In a poem of mine I say that communism and the Kingdom of Heaven are the same. This faith sustains me both as a Christian and as a Revolutionary. I believe in God's Reign, that is — equality — as well as I believe in the social revolution. The expression "Kingdom of Heaven" in Jesus's time meant exactly what the word revolution means now. It was equally subversive. The prophets had announced a new reign but it wasn't subversive since it was to be in the future. Subversive is announcing that it will happen in the present, as Jesus did, and they killed him.

AW: Do you see religious conflict as inevitable?

EC: It's inevitable as long as we have religions. I am against religion. On a trip I made to Chile in Allende's time I met a revolutionary priest who told me that religion was harmful and that a time will come when religion won't be necessary. He compared humanity to a twelve year old girl which I've written about in *Cosmic Canticle*. She is capable of living alone but still is not yet a woman. Humanity is still in its adolescence, not wanting religion. Later this teen will become a woman and will feel the need. But right now humanity doesn't feel like it needs God. But like the girl whose body is developing, the need will come. This was a mystical teaching he gave me. It's not that we need to rid the world of religion, but it will pass naturally:

> The 12 year old girl feels independent.
>> In that tiny hotel in Santiago de Chile.
>> Fr Cortés came in, a religious in the MIR; armed
>> and semi-clandestine although it was in Allende's day.
> The 12 year old girl believes she can live on her own
>> he tells me in that modest little hotel,
>> expounding atheism to me.

She's forsaken dolls now but she's still not a woman.
One day her body will mature and she'll feel incomplete.
That's when the Bridegroom will come.

. . .

Once she played with dolls, listened to fairy tales,
relied on mummy and daddy. That was religion.
Now she feels she can go it alone,
wants to be independent.
The priority: that the girl should develop.
The priority is the Revolution. Still
there are only human beings, not Humanity.
   Fr Cortés's point in the Chilean hotel.
Some sexual cells mature earlier,
feel the need for union earlier.
The hermit is also revolutionary.
   That was in 1971. He died in battle after the coup.

FROM: "Cantiga 40"

Prophets from the Bible taught that God didn't want religion to be like a
cult with sacrifices, incense, altars. God wants the liberation of the op-
pressed. Christ didn't present himself as a religious figure or cult leader. He
was a lay person. He wasn't a priest as in the tribe of Levi. He didn't go to
the temple to pray or perform sacrifices. The Church didn't have priests
until three centuries after his death. One of the fathers of the church said,
boasting to the pagans, that Christians don't have priests, temples nor al-
tars. We have to get back to this primitive church as it is in the Acts of the
Apostles: a fraternal society without rich and poor, everyone receiving ac-
cording to [his] needs. There are similar teachings in other religions, as in
Islam.

There is an ancient Sufi parable that says there are many ways to go to Mecca. You can go South if you are in the North (I guess in Afghanistan). And you can go North if you are in the South, you can go West and you can go East. Every religion leads to God, even atheism. This is an important teaching.

I myself consider religion harmful because it divides humanity. Muslims consider the Holy War a metaphor. A war against ourselves. In Algeria, a Muslim theologian said that in the Koran there are archaic things such as polygamy, women's oppression and holy war, and that these things had to be changed. And they hanged him.

AW: If your former teacher, the great contemplative Trappist Thomas Merton, were alive today, do you think he would recommend retreat or social action?

EC: Both things, there is no contradiction between them.

AW: How does your poetry sustain you?

EC: Poetry doesn't sustain me. Faith does. Faith also sustains my poetry.

SOURCE:
Cardenal, Ernesto, *Cosmic Canticle*, translated by John Lyons, Curbstone Press, 2002.

5 Female Poets Next to a Block of Ice

(— Wrestle the damn dream down!)
                    — ELENI SIKELIANOS

This was the dream
where I left the palm and stereo at home
left my fatigues at home
I became lost in a Theater of Reading
I was provoked by aggressive how-to book titles bobbing out at me
            as I passed the (fluctuating) shelves
"Incapably Positive Chronicles"
"Received Ideas But In No Things Received"
"The President Is Not Projective Thirst You Can Be Too"
"My Hands Are Tongue-Tied"
"More Than Laura Riding Knows"
I open a volume, hands shaking but my condition ordered me to salute
Heil!
I felt like Queen Mab, I wanted to eat nightshade
and ply the spirits of poesia out of their caves
My sisters — all four of them — reminded me of
the Library in Alexandria — think of it before it's sacking
— (time is a spiral)
and suggested how one might behave
            in such a place —
such a Memory Palace, you need, girlfriends, to bow
Joanne was seen polishing marble
Diane remained in samadhi

Alice had her glasses on to scrutinize a miniature map
Eleni was eager for the card catalogue, she started "And you?"
She was *enceinte*, she held the future in a book
I was a lumpen proletariat, a deadbeat, a shaman
I wanted him, the only librarian in the room (snap fingers)
to be a nurturing woman librarian
The world was askew how get it right again?
Stacks of glassine Duncan, Olson thin, weathered Ginsberg,
his pages long with hair
It was "all about" Spicer's grail, the Enron scandal
It was all about death in war, torture
The empire of reading was clear
You needed special glasses provided by Homeland Security
But here there was no "home," there was no "secure"
But something was going to change, get born.

The Essence of Progress is Human

NOTES INVESTIGATING THE POETRY AND POETICS OF ADONIS
CUNY CONFERENCE, NOVEMBER 4, 2005

When there is no poetry in a period of history,
there is no true human dimension.
                                                  — Adonis

Adonis (Ali Ahmad Said), 2005
PHOTOGRAPH: THE AMERICAN
UNIVERSITY IN CAIRO

We need to acknowledge, as Adonis re-
minds us, that poetry is the place to go for
the history, and the concomitant human
dimension that interprets the history. What
else can we trust but poetry?

But there are difficulties in the vexed and
freighted history of poetry, in the master
versions versus the subterranean visions,
the marginalized "others" of little ink and
audience. In a country that has no "use"
for it, understands it — rightly — as
thorny, controversial, against the grain,
imagination in many quarters is suppressed.
Unlike the rich tradition of a poetics going
back many centuries, such as pre-Islamic Persian with a modicum of "un-
broken lineage" albeit with interventions, the rebellion here (the US front)
has been short-sighted — standard verse culture's left hand margin up
against Projective verse, lyrical and self-consumed versus the "eschewing
of the "I" of personal history(confession), or Documentation versus Ap-
propriation. Yet Adonis reminds us of the dilemma in his own culture, in

his own language — the problems of modernity — greater battles than ours, more interesting perhaps, philosophical, going back many centuries . . . the separation of poetry and thought, or knowledge, in pre-Islamic poetry, other penetrating concerns.

Arab thought conditioned by religion, the notion of a solid "Arabness" of language deemed a heap of words . . .

Adonis speaks of the "double siege" of the Arab poet who is dependent on the feudal past but also by a contemporary "culture of dependency." The "modern" of the west being both a lure and perhaps a betrayal. "Modern" for Arab poetics, begins in the 8th century . . . And so on . . .

I've been considering one continuing eidolon on this home turf — the "fictions of whiteness" — this terrorizing legacy, this maintained "fiction" or activity which "syncretically" rubs up against American political hegemony as well. And the suffering of so many denizens on this planet affected by the incursions, assaults, and maintenance of habitually patterned fossil fuel lifestyle and greed of those "fictions." Suffering beings — the Others — who are anything but white. I thought I'd done with this but it keeps coming back as this country currently reels more desperately in its contradictions. What is the relationship to other, "other" which is not a fiction? Is European-American West now the scary "other?"

In 1967 Adonis wrote:

"We no longer believe in Europe. We no longer have faith in its political system or in its philosophies . . . Europe for us — backward, ignorant, impoverished people — is a corpse."

And here we have a governance that hides its prey, its corpses in Iraq, and Abu Ghraib and Guantánamo and criminally neglects its own in New Orleans until the bodies are exposed for the world to see?

For white mongrels Europe is presumably the lineage until we get to Whitman — are we feeding off corpses of the canon or an old fiction? Too many corpses, everywhere . . .

> A corpse this, which confuses the flesh for the garment
> A corpse this, reclined as a book not as ink
> Corpse this, which does not live in the morphology of the body
> nor its garment

FROM: "A Grave for New York"

For Adonis the opposition is not poetical, however:

> Consciousness of the other assumes a realization on our part that the opposition between the Arab-Islamic East and the European-American West is not of an intellectual or poetic nature, but it political and ideological, originally a result of Western imperialism.

FROM: "Poetics and Modernity"

How does a poetics needing to engage politically extend to endangered, as well as "consociational" (note: this is term used by anthropologist Clifford Geerst to indicate the complexity of relationship within a given time frame, given that every individual is on his or her own time cycle) "other" — there — everywhere. Occasions *are* everywhere and one senses it will be the spiritual practices, the visualization of other, the poetry in exchange with "other" that might redeem, save us.

I remember zones fraught with danger, out of my poetic control. Exiting a plane at gunpoint in Beirut during the Six-Day War, arrested at Rocky Flats, held for hours by the *altiferas* in San Andreas de Lorianzar in Chiapas. Or traveling by bus into Iran, with rucksack, your passport is withheld, you are coerced to pay a fee (this is under the Shah), bribes at the Yugoslavian border and so on . . .

How does poetry protect you? How does a poetics of conscience, witness, rage sustain your daily struggle?

One considers the role of poet a privileged niche in some quarters. In others you are nothing, you are dust, you are one of the rabble, you are one of the oppressors. You enter a safe haven or in my case you create an alternative safe haven (The Jack Kerouac School at Naropa University, co-founded with Allen Ginsberg in 1974) — a university — you are safe in the professionalism of your calling. You are often in such contexts to com-ment upon, to muse, to expound on the exigencies of the phoneme, the hypertext, the "phatic function." When we are done with communication, will we prolong the conversation virtually? Isn't it crucial to question a poetics of privilege?

I found myself dismayed to be at a conference recently at a reputable US university, a conference white, western-oriented, avant garde, post-modern in sway. And wonder why we persist in living this fiction, upholding it so tenaciously or unconsciously. I remember that this institution also has one of the first academic Departments of Homeland Security, instituted just two years ago. You might train in racial profiling, among other things.

That is why this gathering at CUNY is welcome, and a particularly heart-ening occasion as we gather here tonight in "a human universe" to honor and hear the poetry of a great humanitarian poet born in a so-called "rogue state" (Syria), who has examined the "constant present" his whole life.

> The road and the house love me
> The living and the dead
> The red jug
> At home
> Its waters in love with it
> The neighbor loves me
> The field and the threshing floor
> The fire
> The arms that toll
> Happy with the world
> or unhappy
> the tear my brother shed
> hidden by the crop
> Anemone that mortifies the blood
> I have been here as long as the god of love
> What would I do if I died

FROM: "Love"

When will a more comprehensive poetics shatter this illusory edifice of dominance? It seems to be happening as things fall apart and the willful totalitarian center cannot hold. Of course "field poets"(as in field notes and I'd also like to invoke Robert Duncan's "opening of the field" here) and cultural workers know the score and are engaged in cross-cultural exchanges, crucial translation projects, correspondences, even as journalist covering war on troubled homefronts. I think of Kalamu ya Salaam, embedded *griot* poet of New Orleans and his documentary project (to record stories of flood victims) in which everyone is invited to partake. He recommends we consider all the afflicted communities of the *polis*. Include the Vietnamese from East New Orleans — at least 12,000 made homeless and "refuge-ed" twice in the past three decades. This was below the radar in first run news reportage, also the Native American communities afflicted by hurricane Katrina.

The range of poetics on this part of the continent is immense, palpable, exciting — whether lyrical, investigative, performative, yet what power does it have to end the war . . . When is it the poet's turn?

> Whitman. Let it be our turn now. I make a ladder of my gaze.
>
> I weave
> My steps into a pillow, and we shall wait. Man dies but he is more
> Eternal than the grave. Let it be our turn now. I wait for the Volga
> To flow between Manhattan and Queens. I wait for the
>
> Hwang Ho to
> Empty where the Hudson empties. Are you surprised? Did the
> Orontes not flow into the Tiber? Let it be our turn now. I hear a
> Convulsion and a roar of thunder. Wall Street and Harlem
>
> meet—leaves
> meet the thunder, dust meets the tempest. Let it be our turn now.

FROM: "A Grave for New York"

How can you be excited by a poem when over 55,000 Pakistanis have just lost their lives tragically for lack of the basic human dignities of nourishment, shelter, medical care —

The fiction of power continues — the manufacturing of consent contin-ues just as the fiction of this unjust war in "othered" Iraq continues. People suffer and die in this fiction.

> And I confess: New York, in my country the curtain and the bed,
> the chair
> And the head are yours. And everything is for sale: the day and the
> Night, the black Stone of Mecca and the waters of the Tigris. I
> Announce: in spite of this you pant, racing in Palestine, in Hanoi, in
> The North and the South, in the East and the West, against people
> Whose only history is fire,
> And I say: ever since John the Baptist, everyone of us carries his severed
> Head in a tray and awaits a second birth.

FROM: "A Grave for New York"

I find myself thirty years after the American war in Vietnam still coming to terms with that history and know I need to include it in the writing because it was my generation's war. I felt extremely welcome as a poet in Vietnam. I went as a pentitent, someone begging forgiveness. There were few citizens my own age, most of them having been destroyed in war. A whole generation wiped out. Many youth born after the war, many maimed and gnarled old men. And things Vietnamese, the people, the lan-guage, the mores entered the West through war through occupation. Cross genre cuisines . . .

Hmong people fishing for bass in the Saw Hill Ponds in Boulder, Colorado . . .

How, I wonder, will Iraq fare in this? *Coming after*? How many soldiers re-

turn with language, truly knowledgeable of another's culture? Very few.
The Marines sit in their bubble worlds, isolated, paranoid, nervous about
their armor. Not welcomed, not wanted. *Go home, get out now.*

Will I visit Iraq as a penitent?

A small minority — at least 7 million or so Muslim adherents — dwell
here on this complicated turf (half Arab-Americans) and are taken to task
to do duty for all Muslims and answer to the state having our "white"
America under terrorist siege. Islam continues to be profiled as anathema
to the white west. Those Americans who might know Arabic to help
crack the terror "codes" — who studied language were suspect, different,
They might even be gay!

But the fiction goes on. Out of touch with the time. A manipulated
fiction. The plight of the Palestinians for many years not even in the
discussion.

And these lines from "Unintended Worship":

> His soul hates wars
> Yet his body loves destruction.
> He used to mutter to himself:
> The sky to the stars
> The earth to the stones
> Where do you fit, you who resemble me
> You they call human?
> ... indeed, history thinks with its feet and here it is, laboring
> to remain
> afloat from stone to stone

here it is perishing like stunned birds
hissing by locked windows
delirious and about to faint. . .

("I hunt among stones" the poet Charles Olson wrote.)

For many of us now, New York City is psychologically the safest site in America. We speak of New York as its own country. It affords a shelter against the *schadenfreude* of our daily existence, the daily psy ops. It can also be occupied — as it was during the Republican National convention — with armed guards, surveillance helicopters, and infiltrated by agent provocateurs. But the underground grows, persists, ancillary to the normative rules of engagement. New York is rife with hybridity — the margins where cultural differences come into play and in Homi Babha's analysis "unsettle all the stable identities that are constructed around oppositions such as past and present, inside and outside, inclusion or exclusion." We need to celebrate the "in between" spaces created and inhabited by hybrids. Class, race, gender are the primary categories, let's continue to deconstruct their shackles even as we inhabit the Third World War:

    1. Space is measured in units of cages or walls
    2. Time is measured in units of ropes or whips
    3. the regime that builds the world is the one that begins
       by killing its brother

FROM: "A Grave for New York"

At the end of his lecture "Poetics and Modernity in An Introduction to Arab Poetics," Adonis writes most eloquently, further opening the field:

If Arabic poetic modernity is partly based on the liberation of what has been suppressed — that is, on the expression of desire — and on everything that undermines the existing repressive norms and values, and transcends them, then ideological concepts like "authenticity," "roots," "heritage," "renaissance" and "identity" take on different meanings. Traditional notions of the continuous, the coherent, the one, the complete, are replaced by the interrupted, the confused, the plural, the incomplete, implying that the words between words and things are constantly changing, that is, there is always a gap between them which saying or writing the words cannot fill. This unbridgeable gap means that the questions "What is knowledge?" "What is truth?" "What is poetry?" remain open, that knowledge is never complete and that truth is a continuing search.

As a frightening, ongoing and familiar militancy — "the eternal war" — continues to play out its strange karmic destruction on the planet and its myriad denizens. Poets need to keep a fluidity with their "cultural interventions," in their role as interlocutors, archeologists of morning, of perpetual inquiry. Adonis in his prodigious work as poet, scholar, historian, translator and philosopher reminds of this most forcefully in his profound consideration of the human.

The word for "earth" at the beginning of the Indo-European language thousands of years ago was *Dhghem*. From this word simply meaning "earth" came the word "humus," the generous handiwork of soil bacteria. And *humble, human, humane*. Is there perhaps a philological parable here?

We often quote William Carlos Williams' (at the Jack Kerouac School at Naropa University):

unworldly love that has no hope of this world and cannot
change the world to its delight

The Bodhisattva-like urge toward "unworldly love" motivates poets such
as Adonis — propels them to move the century forward a few inches to-
ward delight, toward Other, toward the Human.

["A Grave for New York" brought me specifically to some of this
thinking and notation.]

SOURCES:
Adonis, *An Introduction to Arab Poetics*, translated by Catherine Cobham,
Sagi Books, London, 2003.

Adonis, *A Time Between Ashes and Roses*, translated by Shawkati M. Toorawa,
Syracuse University Press, 2005.

Adonis, *If Only the Sea Could Sleep*, editors: Kamal Boullata and Mirene Ghossein,
Green Integer Books, 2002.

from / Iovis 3

gap for
making
in sound,
sound that is made
mum,
not substitute nor word
nor play to range the
mind's obfuscation
'round

bardo is called it
in another realm

resolves in gap
kind chasm a
younger sister
chance
betters intention often
then
if kind can be said to be kin
then smokes
(smolders?)

in clean
love's chance
insulate a chasm —
gape before the
ordinary thing or word
open mouth before a
        break
or
break
through
compression's break —
consciousness
free of body's harm

not meaning noise
but sound's silence
breaks through her
cage
the lotus position

(who is a man not caged
who is a woman not whirr?)

Who Is Sounding?
Gap, Silence, Cage: Lorine Niedecker

LORINE NIEDECKER: A CENTENARY CELEBRATION, 2003
MILWAUKEE & FORT ATKINSON, WISCONSIN

Time is nuttn in the universe.
— LN, letter to Zukofsky

A contemplative "take" suggests ways of extending the look at Lorine Niedecker's writing-mind and encourages a discussion around "view" in the spiritual sense, as well as performance/orality (both public and supremely private), and "silence." I also propose a poetic affinity between the seemingly diametrically opposed Niedecker and Zen-ist John Cage.

Invoked here is the practice of "ti bot," of *sounding* from Asian poetics, referring specifically in the Thai tradition to the striking of a gong, and extended to include the sounding/unlocking/activating of a poem or text. The poem is not activated until it is "struck." This idea relates as well to a sense of text as "rune" or " seed syllable." "Ti bot" sounds in the mind, a kind of inner space as it also may sound out loud in the world. As such it provides a gap, a dis-junct, an intervention, a cutting into the scape.

Niedecker's work is runic, gnomic, koan-like. A koan (a *kong-an*, literally a "public case") — as practiced in Japanese Zen Buddhism is both a riddle, and a psychological/philosophical device, not intuited by usual logics. It is an exercise of attention, a mental posture, a sharp nudge to perception where suddenly the mind holds myriad thoughts (sounds, images, emotions) simultaneously. Not unlike the state of "negative capability" or *satori*. Haiku is intended to do this; poetry may often do this.

There is a gap between Niedecker's logopoeic lines, her clusters. Gap means a place "between" thoughts, the life and death of a thought, between lives, between the places and states of mind one inhabits, often an ur-utterance.

Niedecker has the *siddhi* (accomplishment) of the haiku form. Leaps of imagination, and idea as well as sound. Gap is *bardo*. Groundless. Body-less consciousness. How does one get from here to there and what moves between? The "heaven, earth, man" principle of Japanese haiku involves a practice which relates to fissure, gap, leap, disjunctive association. A practice in Buddhism — *tamal gyi shepa*, which refers to "gap" or leap of mind — concerns cultivating an attitude of co-emergent thinking ("both both"). It essentially encourages a salutary point of view. One is supposed to "drop" conditions and projections in order to rest in the magic of ordinary mind, and in the duality of experience. While not wanting to presume too much of a stretch here towards eastern modes, structures, praxes (a personal bias), I would like to position/imagine Niedecker as poet with *that kind of mind* and refer to the poems influenced directly by Japanese haiku, and her naturally meditative bent. So many poets play off the haiku. Spin-offs include the cinquain, Robert Kelly's lunes, Amiri Baraka's "lo-ku." Cid Corman, Jack Kerouac, others.

John Cage, considered a supreme avant gardist, could rest in the ambiguity of silence. His structures are more radical, closer in a sense to Niedecker's earlier (and at times) riskier, messier surrealist phrasings. How does one measure "gap?" How is one treated with the dynamics of "ordinary mind?" Or with what one knows of history, dream, emotion? Or the modernist agenda, for that matter.

Position Niedecker and Cage in a similar post-transcendentalist mode. They are liberated both in the sense of their spiritual "view" — an attitude that sees the emptiness and playful quality in the phenomena of all conditioned things, including *words* and *sounds* — and in a secular view that is grounded, local, in the world. The position is politically and intellectually liberal, not religious. These views do not conflict with but rather cohere with the non-theism of Buddhism. Both revel in a realm that is considered magical and mysterious in that it cuts through pretension and the grasping toward rigid identity. You would not hear these writers mutter about finding their "voice."

The voice of each is exploratory. Untamed yet disciplined. It catches the nuances of active reading. Documentary poetics on the one hand, and then a precise emptying out on the other. Both folksy. With modest decorum. One imagines each one of them humble, bowing.

Like Cage, Niedecker is never passive, dreamy or "other-worldly." She is very much of this world: inquisitive, minding, albeit from a distance. But she has a cast of mind accepting of suffering, and an aspiration toward "bigger mind." In the poems, in her observations. She lifts from her reading and study and intuits a view that life does not end with the death of the body. How radical is that?

In a letter to Louis Zukofsky dated April 29/45:

> Reading Diderot: Interpreter of Nature. This is what I could have used long ago, alongside Engels and while I was wondering what Emerson was getting at. A great many of my questions are suddenly answered. I really begin to believe that there is another life for us after we die, one not like ours, at least not for a long, long

time. Elements for awhile before we again become, if we ever do, another mass. Time is nuttn in the universe. The elephant may be on his way to becoming a worm, and vice versa, as a species, I mean. All of which I wanted to say in my poem and didn't quite.

FROM: *Niedecker and the Correspondence with Zukofsky*

Jenny Penberthy notes that Niedecker refers most likely to the poem "Look Close," a koan-like poem, which reads:

Look close
the senses don't get it all
a few hundred thousandths of a centimeter
in wave length and you see the mark
or you don't

FROM: *Collected Works*

How does one "see?" How close — how microscopic — can you really get with the senses? What then is looking/knowledge? How steely and absolute is her "or you don't?" Getting "it,"— seeing the mark — is the "ti-bot" or striking of both the sound and the sense. The poem except for "senses," "hundred thousandths," and "centimeter," is monosyllabic, sharp.

Niedecker had read Thoreau in the mid-1930s, sending Zukofsky notes on her reading. From March, 1956:

Dear Louie:
I'm all right. [ ] I take down not my bible but Marcus Aurelius and follow up with Lucretius and Thoreau's Journal (The Heart

of) and why couldn't somebody like Thoreau — a whole family of him — have ever settled here near me?

FROM: *Niedecker and the Correspondence with Zukofsky*

And from June 1st, 1958:

Cleaning the old cupboard I placed three books together that mean most to me —Marcus Aurelius, Thoreau's *Walden* and Japanese Haiku and standing beside them is *Test of Poetry*.

FROM: *Niedecker and the Correspondence with Zukofsky*

Referring to "typing notes on religion," she lists Thoreau along with Leibniz, Plato, Santayana, others.

The Chinese poet Li Po makes an appearance in a poem that braids together several levels of experience and time:

Swept snow, Li Po,
by dawn's 40-watt moon
to the road that hies to office
away from home.

Tended my brown little stove
as one would a cow — she gives heat.
Spring — marsh frog-clatter peace
breaks out.

FROM: *Collected Works*

You have the quotidian "swept snow" (does the snow look swept or has "she" or Li Po swept it?) meeting the two beats of "Li Po," five if you count the comma as a beat. A common image in dharma practice is that of "sweeping," meaning *sweep the mind of distraction*. The modern moon bulb and "office" intersect with the classical poet, and the "road." In a landscape that is both outside and inside, there is the descriptive meditative Asian landscape — dawn, moon, frog, road, peace — these are all tropes of Asian poetries. "Marsh frog-clatter peace / breaks out" is a line of sounding, surprise much like the frog in Basho's pond. We hear a range of o's: "snow," "Po," "moon," "road," "office," "home," "brown," "stove," "cow," "frog." Think of Allen Ginsberg's onomatopoetic pop Basho he would sing like a rap song, embellishing:

> Old pond
> the frog jumps in
> *kerplunk!*

In the mid-1950s, after writing "Poems for Paul," Niedecker worked extensively with what Penberthy calls her "astringent condensed haiku form."

> In the transcendence
> of convalescence
> the translation
> of Basho

FROM: *Collected Works*

Note its repeating s's hissing and slushing in the mouth: trans, -scend, -scence. What is the translation referred to? Is it like Bottom's "I am translated?" Does the translation of Basho provide transcendence to the invalid or one convalescing?

Absent the first word "sky," which is read as title, another 17-syllable poem:

Sky
in my favor

to fly
to downtown crowds
home

and Basho
on my mind

FROM: *Collected Works*

Here is "Basho" again, as one would say "Shakespeare," "Dante," "Blake," or "Sappho" "on my mind." With "my kind of mind," as Ted Berrigan put it once. Or as one might invoke a lover or a state — "Georgia on my mind." Basho took the long road north fleeing crowds. This is a reversal, flying to crowds.

Alliance

Hunger
with a wonder

Mites wintering
in rabbits' ears

Pronuba
    with yucca

Basho's
    backwater

moon-pull
    He was full

at the port
    of Tsuruga

FROM: *Collected Works*

Here the poet identifies with Basho — his backwater is as her own
perhaps. And later in an echo of the former poem, Basho is like the
full moon. The sound is glorious, rich, strange: "Hunger"/ "wonder"/
"Mites/ "rabbits"/ "Pronuba"/ "yucca" / "pull"/ "full"/ "Tsuruga."
The pauses between the clusters each a heartbeat, a universe.

Basho

beholds the moon
    in the water

He is full

at the port
    of Tsuruga

FROM: *Collected Works*

A credit here: Niedecker had a link to Japanese poetries through the deep study and translation work of primary correspondent Cid Corman. (See Corman's translation of Basho's travel journals, *Oku-No-Hosomichi*, published by Ecco in 1968 as *Back Roads to Far Towns*.)

Now compare/contrast some of Niedecker's "poethics" and practices to those of John Cage. And while they never encountered one another and no record of any response to their respective work either way exists, although Niedecker had a copy of *Silence* in her library, there is room for such a poetic mating. Of course their differences are considerable, especially in terms of individual personae. Cage is the public person — a celebrated international figure, who traveled the world as composer and poet both. He worked collaboratively, creating and performing scores for Merce Cunningham. Niedecker, on the other hand, refused offers to read in public, stayed close to her roots and lived a life at a remove from the avant-garde, albeit none the less rich and complex. She made fun of Ian Hamilton Finlay's offer to have a folk guitar accompany her reading of her poetry for a tape recording.

Her refusal to tour and give public readings of her poetry even extended to her resistance to this idea of recording herself on tape. Cid Corman recorded her shortly before she died, but the reading is brief. She would not project her verse in the impersonal manner it required. "I fell over one of the stanzas and nearly squashed it," she explained in a letter to Kenneth Cox.

The strongest direct link with Cage may well be Thoreau whom they both admired. Thoreau's clarity, modesty, near folksy wit and bare bones lifestyle was appealing. A "rugged individualism" and meditative spirit as well. Disciplined and exuberant. For Niedecker, he was a Yankee predecessor living in the woods in relative isolation, communing intimately with the natural world. It was important to Cage that Thoreau had invented the pencil.

"Each day his eyes and ears were open to see and hear the world he lived in"(*Empty Words*). Lines of Niedecker seem apt here:

> I was the solitary plover
> a pencil
>   for a wing-bone
> From the secret notes
> I must tilt

FROM: *Collected Works*

Indeed the Transcendentalist might have been a good neighbor to both, comparing notes on minute particulars, stalking the edible mushrooms.

Cage was fond of quoting Thoreau. In the "Tenth Interview" (with Richard Kostelanetz), Thoreau's *Journals* is on his list of ten favorite books. Thoreau figures in many of his chance operations. He wrote "through Thoreau" and quoted him often.

"The best communion of men happens in silence"

"simplify, simplify"

"Reading the Journal (Thoreau's)," Cage says, "I had been struck by the twentieth-century way Thoreau listened. He paid attention to each sound — explored the neighborhood of Concord." Thoreau provided Cage with music, silence, and sound. Cage records the sounds through his piece "Mureau." "Mu" from music.

Cage writes: "Silence like music is non-/existent. There always are sounds. That/is to say if one is alive to hear them."

Thoreau's *Walden* starts out with his chosen condition of separateness, a Zen retreat mode, then moves/pushes, even accelerates into an intimacy with the busy world. Meditation in Buddhism, ironically, is seen as a *link* to other sentient beings — all the denizens of the planet which include the "trees and greenery and so on," as one Buddhist chant puts it. One's meditation includes the entire pulse of cyclical existence. It engenders empathy with the world, with the suffering of "other," rather than retreat from. But to accomplish this "right view" as it is called, one needs hours of solitary retreat and practice, being attentive to the *ayatanas* or the *awakened* senses as well as the subtle shifts of the mind. Where do thoughts come from? Where do they go?

The gap is a moment when the "watcher" or "ego," the manipulator, lets down guard. Gap is seen as a powerful meditation praxis. It is a moment when body speech and mind are synchronized, and when there is no ownership of experience. This stopping of grasping mind is the purpose of the *koan*. The writing of both Niedecker and Cage in many aspects functions in this zone, as does Basho's. The transcendentalists had posited intuition over scientific rationalism. "Trust thyself," said Emerson, relying on direct experience. Niedecker and Cage seem consummate post-transcendentalists.

Niedeckers's personal life in terms of issues of *literal* gap and silence is also relevant perhaps. Think of the ways she was compromised in the relationship with Zukofsky — their early love affair, her pregnancy and subsequent abortion. These conditions demanded suppression — a palpable emotional pressure, and in spite of elisions, a "sounding" tension. In fact, the elisions create a greater tension for the reader. Inside the gap exists her love, her hunger, her debt as she perceives it, to Zukofsky. What's seen/ what's unseen is a powerful bifurcation. We understand — fissure has been a particular focus for many of us of late in the current social/political/cultural realm and often personal realm — the body, its broken health and heartbreak. And yet keeping the wit and longer view, Niedecker writes:

> You with sea water running
> in your veins sit down in water
>   Expect the long-stemmed blue
>   speedwell to renew
>   itself

FROM: *Collected Works*

"a person conscious of a listening audience would write just a tiny bit differently"

FROM: *Collected Works*

>   *silence*
>   different-ed
>   taut, or listen
>   silence cracks
>   the pattern of silence
>   broke   fist?

[] [] [] [] [] []

        I needed you
            & I needed
    your
    sound
    on deck

    Anne Waldman, FROM: *Iovis 3*

"Niedecker's idea of the silence of the reader waiting to be filled is evoca-
tive because it underlines the importance of sound to her poetry, and her
lack of the recognition onto which poets can project relations between
poem and reader from within the poem itself," writes Peter Middleton in
his essay "Lorine Niedecker's 'Folk Base'and her Challenge to The Ameri-
can Avant-Garde."

In a letter to Cid Corman on May 3, 1967, she described the audience at a
reading she attended as "mixed and nerve-crossed . . . somewhat inatten-
tive" and said she would only be able to manage if she could find a way
that "the silence could be governed among the people."

Middleton continues in his essay: "The silence is an absence of dialogue, of
conversation, due to the distance between poet and reader. Her poem be-
gins there, with this silence, this absence of inter-subjectivity, rather than
immediately appealing to the universalizing languages and frameworks of
modern art and the avant-garde. This is why she is explicit (in the letter to
Corman) about the intimate scale on the intersubjectivity with which her
poetry aims to work. 'Poems are for one person to another, spoken thus, or
read silently.' This is a poetry that refuses the blandishments that promise it

can be placed anywhere in public culture without loss, and does not be-
lieve that it can always put other people's thoughts into words without at-
tenuation."

One has the irony of "silence" and the intervention of "silence," the spiri-
tual need for silence, and the interruption of silence. John Cage, of course,
was acutely aware of the "noise," which fills the silence of our projects, our
history, our lives, our very existence. And he worked in musical modes,
oral modes, performative strategies involving chance operation, homage,
strategies that worked with the mystery and literal ticking of time. How
opposite to Niedecker's praxis, one might ask?

Most interesting is what they share: they both wrote across genres and, in
Cage's case, across art forms. They were both naturalists, both attentive
and "minding" the details. Ornithology. Bird song. She wrote to the "twit-
tering and squawking noises from the marsh." The soundscape of her is-
land. They share methods of appropriation, fissure, homage, song. They are
both "looking around in America" through text, history. Both politically
progressive, interested in social reform. Niedecker touches on the Depres-
sion, World War II, incipient fascism, the atom bomb. Cage — a citizen of
the world — speaks about breathing in our lives more "anarchistically."

Some of Niedecker's earlier chattier poems invoke both Gertrude Stein
and Cage's original anecdotal story-telling.

> Old Hamilton hailed the man from the grocery store:
> What's today, Friday? Thursday? oh,
> nothing till tomorrow.

FROM: *Collected Works*

Cage says:

"I write/ in order to hear; never do I hear/then write what I hear"

and

　　　　...It is not
　　　　. . . .
　　　　in the nature of doing to
　　　　. . . . .
　　　　improve but rather to come
　　　　. . . . .
　　　　into being, to continue, to
　　　　. . . . . .
　　　　go out of being and to
　　　　. . . . . .
　　　　be still, not doing. That
　　　　. . . . .
　　　　still not–doing is a
　　　　. . . . .
　　　　preparation. It is not
　　　　. . . . .
　　　　just static: it is quiet
　　　　. . . . . . .
　　　　readiness for whatever and
　　　　. . . . . . .
　　　　the multiplicities are already
　　　　. . . . .
　　　　there in the making. We watch
　　　　. . . . .

Lorine Niedecker at Black Hawk Island, Wisconsin, 1967
PHOTOGRAPH BY BONNIE ROUB

for signs and accept omens, so
. . . . . .
we continue doing and changing.

FROM: *Silence*

How things are overheard is important to both of them. They are both in-side an avant-garde nexus yet expand the possibilities for us of *listening*.

I must possess myself, get back into pure duration,
or I should like to be an orator and rise . . .

FROM: *Collected Works*

Jenny Penberthy states "her work is distinguished by its attentive use of sound — conditioned by poor eyesight, her mother's deafness and immersion in the other sounds of Black Hawk Island."

Beautiful girl
pushes food onto her fork
with her fingers —
        will throw the switches
of deadly rockets?

FROM: *Collected Works*

This is a very loud poem and has the tripartite juxtaposition of haiku.

Critic Gordana P. Crnkovic notes:

The language of silence Cage posits is one that knows how to "listen" when the other centers are acting, so that it may construct itself as a re-action to the other senses, and not only as the self-determined action of its own talking. So silence is not just the absence of talk. It is very much listening to what else is going on. In fact there is no such thing as silence.

An anecdotal aside: I recall a moment when the poetics of "silence" became evident during a visit John Cage made to Naropa University in 1974 when he performed Part 4 of his piece "Empty Words" — a decomposition utilizing chance procedures, which included projected slides of calligraphic drawings from Thoreau's *Journals*. Cage sat with his back to the audience in the dark, a tensor lamp lighting the page. He mouthed, in what seemed like 10 minute-intervals, the text which deconstructs — slows down — gets inside the syllables and consonants of words. Then there were huge gaps of silence for looking at the projections. Because it was the day that President Nixon resigned in huge disgrace, people were in a celebratory — one could almost say anarchistic and atavistic mood — and the event had been billed as a "concert" yet carrying the sense, because it was John Cage, that this would be a participatory event. Young folk were showing up from the entire community of Boulder with guitars, flutes, pots and pans and began joining in as he performed his very slow attentive, focused meditative piece. A visceral tension ensued and reached a breaking point perhaps 20 minutes into the performance when John abruptly turned from his very focused rendering — remember his back was set against us — and lashed out "I thought this was a Buddhist school!" and delivered a polemic on listening — it was about being quiet so we could HEAR the traffic lights change. Anxious at the time — being in charge of the event — I later appreciated the contradictions and the questions it raised about performance, listening, identity and emotional response of the presenter when things are not going the way they expected, the investment in a style, assumptions of both presenter and audience.

Also Thoreau as a *medium* for the time in early-1970s Boulder, Colorado in what was the beginning of an experiment in education, the intervention of politics, the need to explode and "party," dancing on Nixon's tomb so to speak . . . This was a radical pedagogical moment. Cage seemed to be "channeling" Thoreau.

Barbara Guest posits an enticing dynamic on the "positions" of the poet as both viewer and insider where the "I" and "you" become a matrix for the "gap" that could be seen as the poem itself. And that gap is magnetic, free, not just empty. Just as in Buddhism "emptiness" has incredible energy and luminosity. The second position, which assumes some responsibility, is in fact the lotus position, the traditional Buddhist meditative posture.

The person inside a literary creation can be both viewer and insider. The window is open and the bird flies in. It closes and a drama between the bird and its environment begins.

When the person who is you the viewer, you believe an extraordinary strength exists in that position. You are outside the arena of dispute or creativity or blasphemy, dwelling in a private space where emotive speculation is stronger than fact or action, each of which passes before you in an attempt at dissimulation which you are free to dispute. This is called the orchid position, because of the extravagant attention the viewer demands.

Without the person outside there would be no life inside. The scene relies on the exterior person to explain the plangent obsessions with which art is adorned.

Yet inside the window is the person who is you, who are now looking out, shifted from the observer to the inside person and this shows in your work. When you are the inside person you can be both heavy and delicate, depending upon your mood; you have a sense of responsibility totally different from the you outside. You occupy the lotus position.

Barbara Guest, FROM: "Shifting Persona,"
in *Forces of Imagination*

I conjure a lotus posture for Niedecker, inside the work, inside the mind, modest and resolute. The sound of the gong striking. A gaze through gap and silence, a gaze toward "the inscrutable east."

Before my own death is certified,
recorded, final judgement
judged

taxes taxed
I shall own a book
of old Chinese poems

and binoculars
to probe the river
trees.

FROM: *Collected Works*

SOURCES:
Niedecker, Lorine,
Collected Works, edited by Jenny Penberthy, University of California Press, 2002.
Niedecker and The Correspondence with Zukovsky, edited by Jenny Penberthy,
Cambridge University Press, 1993.
Crnkovic, Gordana P., "Utopian America and The Language of *Silence*" in
John Cage, Composed In America, edited by Marjorie Perloff and Charles Junkermann,
University of Chicago Press, 1994.
Cage, John, *Empty Words, Writing '73-'78*, Wesleyan University Press, 1979.
Middleton, Christopher, "Lorine Niedecker's 'Folk Base' and Her Challenge to the
American Avant-Garde," in *The Objectivist Nexus: Essays in Cultural Poetics*, edited by
Rachel Blau DuPlessis and Peter Quatermain, University of Alabama Press, 1999.
Guest, Barbara, *Forces of Imagination (Writing On Writing)*, Kelsey St. Press, 2003.
Waldman, Anne, *Iovis 3*, unpublished.
Kostelanetz, Richard, *Conversing With Cage*, Limelight. 1988.

from / Matriot Acts

Women are the weapons of history, we are the symbolic representations of compassion and decency.
—CARRIE MAE WEEMS

invoke the hyena in petticoats!
laughing hyena, spotted hyena, striped —
all stalk the charnel ground amidst
microscopic & telescopic worlds
a step ahead of what is to come in lineage
in gratitude, in naming *las madres*
les femmes, all those against war
look for reclamation, sniff it out —
in a voice not my own but all of them
the wizened ductile face of slumbering female memory:
beginning of time, the timepiece of time
she who was the mother of a ghost ship
ship-of-locked-awe and subjugated dream
she who could never be reduced to a "gender issue"
she who announced a talismanic bond to planet
who saw vole tracks in the snow once on the
radical poet's tiny death plot
Lorine, Lorine! you can come out now —
and Mina and Hilda and Gertrude of all grammar's mind
who salvaged a blow dryer for the art people while
they sold the rights to textures of paper, of glass

(touch me, touch me with crenellated beauty now)
particles in the sunlight, a democratic grace
who documented hurts and slights & transmuted them
to poetry, to flesh, to the wink after sex
she was a challenge in all my hearts, the penultimate maker
did you have any animals around you from the start? *she asked*
did you enjoy yourself a lot?
how old were you when you started this running around?

Beat Roots

for Bobbie Louise Hawkins

While the Muse holds her head, and the crazy Elementals
    Hold down their wrath
Lightly under the earth's surface.
                    — Joanne Kyger

At fifty below
Fuel oil won't flow.
And propane stays in the tank.
Fire poets
Burn at absolute zero
Fossil love pumps back up.
                    — Gary Snyder

dreamt eternal
        by the Ganges
            a river
        still to be found
            in the interior
                of America
                    — Lawrence Ferlinghetti

Once on the drug, we were traveling, we were in ayahuasca land, we were in the land of brujo and bruja, someone said, "these scarabs get lost around me." It was not the shaman, it was the partner of the painter who took me on a wild goose chase around the moors of Bolinas and I lost the fancy leather coat of one Robert Creeley.

What had we smoked?

Fog, always. A sentinel for some kind of trial, tribulation, death of the psyche. You remember Magda.

You remember Lew Welch had disappeared by then. *A good bird always flies like a vulture* (Milarepa sang).

Someone else had died. Many of the players were still alive.

Prayer flags in the wind to vocalize Tibet in America.

Old Bull Burroughs was in his cups about scorpions how they are clearly he said, *clearly*, repellant. And if anything scared him, they did. Old Bull was recalcitrant in his need for inebriants and the bug-thing was emphatically a part of the lore of poison, anti-dote, of nectar of cum, of blood of the savior. It's all mixed up in lethal fear I think I said. I told of my scorpion bite out on the Egyptian desert, and he winced.

The coat was found in the long a.m. huddled in the corner of that witchy woman's cave.

§

We were eye to eye in our Buddhism with politics, which is why it made sense to mix mantra with political protest and why you could simply mimeo little slips of paper with words like OM AH HUM and mingle them with Freedom and Justice. This was back in the elder Mayor Daly's time. And we circled the Chicago Park, ever alert for the crack of night-stick and we took to sleeping on the wing, vigilant . . . and we sat in the courthouse by day next to the black man activist gagged for the world to see. Bobby Seale, gagged for all the world to see.

Anne Waldman and Allen Ginsberg
(with dancers Barbara Dilley and Douglas Dunn), Naropa, 1975
PHOTOGRAPH BY RACHEL HOMER

And did it? Did it see? Did it see the Fellaheen world?

Judge Hoffman seemed to be in a play by Molière, the rhetoric was inter-
esting. You could forget the part about manacles, jail time. You could forget
that we were trying to bring that war system down. It would come down
thanks to the Viet Cong resisting as we spoke. On the fringe of the park
now, Allen Ginsberg effusive for the fresh air, outside in the gypsy dark,
megaphones, mantra. We would bring the world here to meditate for 24
hours at least and it would be a more sober clear-seeing world. Vipassana
world, all to see. This could this would this might be done.

Earlier Allen had been brought to vatic speech by the enormity and ex-
cesses of power-mad euphemism. Pentagon wake from planet-sleep! Om

Raksa Hum Hum Hum Phat Svaha! He said in so many words in a transmission mode, *You can always match their power in words. Stay candid.*

§

Gregory Corso invaded my shower one day in the little Townhouse apartment I return to in dreams as "Remember Some Apartments." It was named "Emerson Apartments." Ralph Waldo Emerson had always been an inspiration for my memory of this place, although he would not have appreciated the commune spirit. Gregory was always barging in, rooting around looking for valium or anything palliative and high-making, gesticulating, checking out my books — did I have any art books? — and would I ever be as good as Jane Austen? So there was that, the sense of invasion.

I was soaping my hair with lavender shampoo. We decided we would probably never sleep together. That was a good idea because he was so complicated to think about sleeping with. I mean it wasn't even an issue or much of a discussion. I was not going to get my transmissions from Beat poets, I proclaimed, by sleeping with them! I said would you be my pal? And will you behave? He hugged me as we were water rats together in the shower.

§

On the road to the contagious hospital.

It breaks me up, last days of Philip Whalen, I can't tell of it very well. In the years of war, of dark age, all the genocide raining down. Who's in charge? Philip would ask. Not I. "Them." "Them is dead!" Them is an anachronism."

Anne Waldman with Philip Whalen, New York City, 1972
PHOTOGRAH COURTESY OF ANNE WALDMAN ARCHIVES

Let me say. Laguna Honda — "a" hospital — hospital? No, a state of mind perched high but down on its luck, better days, lovely minimally attended gardens, all variety of cactus — is the Bardo. Flashing on his hens and chickens those little swirls of succulents. And "Anne, you don't know how to speak to the chickens, let alone the hens, not like that . . ." (admonishment 1967) . . .

Let me say as we — filmmaker Nathaniel Dorsky and I — walk first in to the empty anteroom we cross a magic threshold. The antechamber to death, to the part where you only have your hearing left and someone is reading *The Tibetan Book of The Dead,* where you fight off flickering projections back to every encounter with our dying Roshi. The time you took his hand. The time he was reading Emily Dickinson and the space got interrupted by the young man having an epileptic fit his pencil swinging madly out of control on the page where he was making notes and Philip kept going. She (Emily Dickinson) could handle that, he said later ... So all these projections arise in the antechamber. I could see Philip thin and fragile, or large and swollen. I could see him with hair and beard and I could see him enjoying food, Chinese food. Take-out. What path would he chose in the Bardo? The bright lights of food and pleasure, the dimmer light of ordinary mind? Or the most challenging blaze of all, dangerous, come back right away and save mankind.

Woe mankind, Allen sang.

And Joanne Kyger has reported in April how Philip called and said he was roaming on Sutter Street without a cent and would someone come and pick him up? His fantasy, twilight mind already taking off.

And she said, *This now is for me how it was for you with Allen.*

One corridor, the patients reaching out to us — can you fetch a glass of water? Light my cigarette? Push my wheelchair into the sun?

It seemed to be a room of Vets from the sixties war.

Philip lying in the hall set up temporarily with other patients while the rooms were being painted, suddenly shiny and luminous. Blind and clear and seeing us. Curtain, gauzes of discretion and intimacy set up between the dying, you hear them breathing. Philip was turning his dharma wheel.

§

We gathered for the
festival in Ostia, the place
where Fellini filmed all the
beach scenes near Rome.
Om pah pah bands
marching the sand, the
boy-child leader allegori-
cally Optimism and
Imagination both. Beauti-
ful chaos set against the
ebb and flow of moon,
time, water, innocence,
impermanence and flicker
of celluloid . . .

Amiri Baraka teaching, Naropa, 1994
PHOTOGRAPH COURTESY OF NAROPA ARCHIVES

The mob had been camp-
ing at Ostia two days. Ex-
tremely hungry, they could
storm the stage! the organizers warned. They had been promised rock n'
roll and food. Strategy meetings. William Burroughs said "A chair is a
weapon. Stand your ground." Allen was conciliatory remembering the
savagery of cops in Chicago. A stoned damsel came to the mic and droned
on for what seemed an eternity her sense of the whole earth and we are
all bellissimo. Ted Berrigan said we should have in our voices the voice of
Mayakovsky reading to a huge stadium of nudniks.

Amiri urged caution — there could be agent provocateurs afoot.
"Be cool." How would the police react? We were being paid in lire "un-

der the table." Our hosts were anarchists. Amiri's intensity a graceful proprioception that when the crowd rushed the stage — it was surely built for this, like a movie set — and we leapt off, I caught his face — resolute, *we've seen this before.* Survival, William had a wooden plank in his hand.

§

I'd been given a gift certificate to Bergdorf's and John Wieners wanted it from the start as there was then a kind of sisterly competition we were playing at which is what I am thinking now. So let's go up there now (then). He was just visiting. And about to give a reading in the gold lamé "number" à la Liberace. A sort of leisurewear pants suit, one pant leg rolled up like a sleeve.

He's wadding gobs of Kleenex into a bra and the salesgirl is being very attentive, playing along and John wants to try on a range of blouses, prolong the agony of decision. By contrast, I am a quick, impulsive shopper. I knew the best on him from the start but he's not buying it. So we end up with a rather dowdy black thing that doesn't look any better back at the apartment on St. Mark's Place as he's primping in front of the mirror, but that means we can go back tomorrow and find another. *That would be best.*

Then I can't remember what happened. But I think this is all before he tries to board the airplane to Rome without a passport and ends up (again) at Wingdale. And one visits the large rooms with mad people in them and he's very distracted and medicated. *Melancholy carries / a red sky and our dreams . . .*

§

Darrell Gray, Bobbie Louise Hawkins, Jim Nisbet, Joanne Kyger,
Donald Guravich, Nancy Vogel, Alastair Johnston (left to right);
front row: Travis, Jesse & Andy Vogel, Santa Barbara, 1979
PHOTOGRAPH BY SHELDON VOGEL

Where was alchemy in 1961? Where was dear Freddie Herko in 1962 be-
fore he walked out the window. And the unguents and libations of velvet
life and stammer and conquest and wow. How many arms can one woman
have to keep a world afloat? And make babies? This bird — my dove —
flies backwards and in all 10 directions of space.

Laboratories and ruminations of the goddess di Prima inhabit The Albert
Hotel. One: a brew of herbal elixirs, good for circulation of the blood.
Two: the mind of the poet that warms to John Dee because he was a seer.
Three: if you could mix sulphur and mercury you would be the perfect

bi-sexual. Four: get on stage and act out a scream to dare the elements of invocation. Five: revolution. Six: the rotundity and science of light and cool. Seven: a place in the country preferably underground. Eight: live outside the system, and forever. Nine: barter on the side. Ten: the upsidedown fool, welcome him.

I wrote some things down for the future to bank upon, to stay the blast. My cards said "obviate," my swords said "rule," my cards said "a sun in your center," my cards said "heartbreak." I started out to walk early in the New York — cool, collected — dawn, her Tarot on my mind.

Joanne was dancing to make the world jump to its swirled attention. Metabolism! Metabolism! There was always Joanne restless in the back unable to take a seat in the establishment of official poetrydom. It is ripped this culture, poets sitting in an auditorium. Let's blow the cover! The wild little girl inside Joanne, elegant in black. Boundaries anathema to Bard Joanne, as she shakes jar of lentils, anything to shake the rattle with this interesting night at hand where you could gab with the moon and her minions. Little spirits that will push back the dawn. The bubble of toil and trouble. How might I ever commune with her spirits — hellbent, radical, freewheeling, conversant spirits? Who will speak me my poetry?

I watched and watch her hear her steady, many years. I hear her quiver and deliver the lines that were closest to the rhythm of her head space grammar. The neurons sparked and charging. We walked on the beach collecting agates. They were the eyes of deities. We swallowed the hard Tibetan long-life pills to obviate the pain of never wanting it to end, go on, go on . . . crazy wisdom . . . gone beyond gone.

Corset

in memory, KATHY ACKER & FOR AMBROSE

what is it to be corset maker binding the bone and cotton in a
daily sweat of labor and purpose what is it to know the sweat of
all you my sister workers of daily living surviving an economic
purse-string purpose what is it to be declared the most dangerous
of purpose when J. Edgar Hoover has your number and what is it
here now in St. Petersburg hungry and anxious and soul-stirring
for surviving my purpose what is the cause of insomniac passion
my further disillusionment in your systems in your many systems
in all the systems that bind the bone in this labor to you who will
always profit off the labor of Emma's hands sewing binding aching
toiling bone and cotton in the class struggle a dangerous purpose
you want to call it that why you can call it that and it's so much
more but do call it that and you will I'm sure call it that and most
dangerous of violence and terror too and what of a Spanish Civil
War I'll call wake up all minions! I'll call: arise! and would cast in
a daily sweat of labor a struggle a sweet edge that way for it's an
energy of daily sweat and toil to be free of the fascisms of how
and when and why and why o never free of J. Edgar Hoover but
my imagination ever free of the imagination of J. Edgar Hoover
who will surely most certainly have your number in his fractious
labor and psychopathic toil even now when he the ghost of
fractious J. Edgar Hoover is stalking haunting the work places the

meeting places the "commune" of all my sweat and purpose —
what is it to a large woman be-speckled and intent in my libertar-
ian socialist moment to incite a riot what is it to be thus called
trouble and to be forever "unpopular with authorities" to be
watched and goaded and arrested and in lock-down what kind of
terror moment is this and will it survive and assassinate a president
this kind of moment will it will it survive McKinley will it
survive psychopathic fractious J. Edgar Hoover and will the ghosts
of Haymarket stalk the Union Hall still in that old purpose and
will that will now sisters break the corset that binds the moment?

Ambrose Bye, Danny Dabiri, and Jason Wahlberg
Anti-war protest, San Francisco, 2002
PHOTOGRAPH BY ANNE WALDMAN

Feminafesto: Olson

FOR OLSON NOW / ST. MARK'S POETRY PROJECT
DECEMBER 2005, & IN PROGRESS

Feminine
   Writing so that all the world
   is redeemed, and history
   and all that politics,
   the "State" and Subjection,
   are for once, done away with,
      as the reason
of writing.

And from "Footnote to HU (lost in the shuffle)":

And the 6'4" Negress stood in the middle of the room full of
bright and talking people. Listened for a moment to what they
were going on about, and threw this at them, as her contribution:
ART IS THE CELEBRATION OF THE ACTUAL. And with-
out giving them a moment to think, said: ONLY THE ARTIST
(she had just come in) IS ON TIME!

The feminine, the goddess (you could say *inside* Olson) winks every-
where. She's all over the place in the field of Olson. *Polis* is goddess's eyes.
Poetry's job is to reclaim the awareness of the world and to be on point,
on time, ready, gestated. Not carrying reference or received un-digested
knowledge. Not lost in ownership of "thing," or of odious comparison of
thing over other thing. Rather embrace self-existence of the natural sym-
bol. Things are symbols of themselves. Language is the instrument we play
on. That's what he got at. AND THE FEMININE WAS THE FEMI-

NINE. Albeit still in "goddess" motif. The feminine as I experience it sees the un-conditionality of space. Of letting things exist or giving them enough silken rope to hang themselves . . . And poetry, as feminine, might be in turn, truly be in turn, the RIVAL GOVERNMENT. And more and more required that it be, this rival zone, a feminine-energy project. Not female. *Feminine*. Feminine in principle which is about container, atmosphere, perspective, community — in the Sanskrit, *prajna* — wisdom of womb-born. *Prajna* also carries a notion of discriminating awareness wisdom. Get over it, guys. Turn in the psychological hung-up non-existent paper tiger WMD! The fiction of white male dominance. It's OVER. "Redeemed," because the feminine out of female for the most part designates the sex which nurtures, does not torture, bears offspring & keeps "it" going. In my experience, also sees — intuitively KNOWS — the interactions, the vibrations of the symbiotic web of life, experience, language. Olson might have been confused, demonized by what dark "un-resolve" was represented by Mother, by Wife, by Lover, by Daughter. The harmony of the universe, he said, is not logical. *Logos is not a final discipline. Instanter and instanter.* Discourses are dodges. Most wanting of illumination and pleasure. The thing itself, and its relevance to ourselves who are the "experiencers" of it, needs liberation. Cut to the chase . . .

If you do this to that, THIS happens, or that to that to that to THAT, that happens. Karma is everywhere in the Big O's mappemunde. History — whose version? you have to ask. Olson's was wild on this: *istorin*, check it out for yourself. You already know, from us Lunarians who spend a lot of time reflecting back your own guys' and your master master-narratives' light, you must be equipped to let it go, the history, the "Subjection," the State. *It's not working.* Towards the end of "Human Universe," Olson parses shape-shifting Mayan myth — How it's better to be a bird, or man and woman as the sun and moon are, or how you can turn into a wasp, a humming bird, or how moon puts on a crab shell in disguise. How the particulars of the protean dance *are* Magic! *Hot for the world they lived in* he says of those (Maya) closer to the earth, the planets . . . Was it a naive romanticism born of privilege? Partially. Although Olson lived in poverty as a poet. Olson turned me toward La Ruta Maya, toward the codices, toward the struggle of the Zapatistas — I thank him. "Communalism and anarchism," that's what needs negotiating as Don Byrd so eloquently points out in a recent essay on Olson "an actual earth of value/to construct one."

What do we need to reclaim as poets, investigators, *archeologists of morning*? What needs to be uncovered? Regrouped? Where indeed is Olson Now? How is Poetry and Olson the good news?

What became a post mortem of Olson was a critique of the life. A dissembling attitude toward his management of Black Mountain. His family's suffering. The poverty. He was another white macho male — bossy, heroic. The work? My god, the enormity of the Creeley correspondence in hand. The Full *Maximus* with Guide to wonder & ponder. Don Allen & Ben Friedlander's *Collected Prose.* The Correspondence with Frances Boldereff so well under Maud & Thesen's competent editorship. Suddenly we had a critique of Mythopoetics (what better in the hands of an Olson?) And anyone who *saw the universe this way* — *magically!* which was a no-no for the Language School. (Perloff had short shrift for O.) That he was an obstacle rather than a boon to women's work. (Yet Olson was also being, streamed through writers one respected — Creeley, Ed Dorn.) The idea of epic as a male form off-limits to serious women writers was referenced in my own case (the *Iovis* Project — now 800 pages). Uncovering of the crucial relationship with Frances Boldereff for the work, thought, investigation. This woman of unique brilliance cast a huge beam on so many of his poetic forays, obsessions. Her letters shine, nurture . . . she is overlooked perhaps in her own right. We shall see.

An apprentice of the New American poetry, as a young woman I saw
Olson at 20. Witnessed him come un-glued then hold fast, an open sys-
tem, a flickering *dissipative structure* at Berkeley. Watched him eschew king-
ship. Falling apart and coming into strange shape in the act of the poem.
The fluidity of the feminine was attractive, albeit ungainly.

Gloucester was the choice for my first marriage's honeymoon. A city that
was a poem. I saw Olson at the famous reading in London, Royal Albert
Hall, his hands pressing assiduously on the podium. Was it an hallucination
his feet hovering about the stage dancing, could that be? I spoke with him
briefly at the famous party with Ungaretti, Michael X and Mick Jagger,
held at Panna Grady's home: the former Chinese Embassy. I said come to
the Poetry Project. I sent him arrowheads as he was dying in New York.

The womanless *Call Me Ishmael* is a wrestle with Ahab's demons, a world
crying out for balance, in need of redress. The readings in poetry, philoso-
phy, history, Shakespeare, are female absent. That's the exploration, where
it took him. It's up to us, *coming after* to raise further issues, the ante, the
bar, extend the conversation. Isn't the mind, the politics, Olson's perspec-
tive often feminine? I have been honoring dead heroes, fathers for
months (as have many of us — for years): Creeley, Berrigan, Olson, Ken-
neth Koch. I spent hours over last weekend being interviewed by Coppo-
la's people for the Kerouac & Beat documentary. The exemplary women
of my generation are elders now — let's get them in the conversation be-
fore they, too, are the dead Mothers we mourn. Olson I think would be
knocked over by the work of Susan Howe, of Bernadette Mayer, of Lyn
Hejinian, Alice Notley. By the long stamina of their poems.

For tasks: Writing by *Women* and *Men*. More trust in our innate Proprio-
ception. Generally, see the history/version of a particular kind of thug
Male. The dead-end State (control) we notice everywhere and inside our

own psyches. How they get into our deepest creative zones as the "reason for writing." Question the rampant subjection, clearly, as in "extraordinary rendition," rendition of humanity, of language, rendition of compassion. The Praxis: out from under an insane hierarchy of grab & Empire & bleak euphemistic language. And a globalization that stinks. All the great heroic ghosts are in us, waiting for the reclamation, redemption for the end of this Subjection, all the crimes of the State. I watched President Truman from my baby carriage as his motorcade snaked in a victory parade after WW II down Houston Street, and was told I cried.

Olson quit that War Information Office job, turned toward the feminine praxis and frequencies of poetry.

Here's a *cento* of sorts:

> And she sprinkled water on the head of the child, crying
> "Cioa-coatl! Cioa-coatl!"
> with her face to the west.

FROM: "The Kingfishers"

•

> What has he to say
> In hell it is not easy
> To know the traceries, the markings
> (the canals, the pits, the mountings by which space
> declares herself, arched, as she is, the sister,
> awkward stars drawn for teats to pleasure him, the brother
> who lies in stasis under her, at ease as any monarch nor
> a happy man

.... how
shall he convert this underbrush, how turn this unbidden place
how trace and arch again
the necessáry goddess?"

                                    And who
Can turn this total thing, invert
and let the ragged sleeves be seen
By any bitch or common character?
Who can endure it where it is, your beloved is, where she
Who is separate from you, is not separate, is not
goddess, is, as your core is,
The naming of one hell

                          Where she moves off, where she is
                          No longer arch

                          That men kill, do kill, that woman kills
                          Is part, too, of his question

FROM: "In Cold Hell, In Thicket"

                              •

Because the human is so light a structure

FROM: "For Sappho, Back"

she rose
from the genital
wave

FROM: "The Ring Of"

•

Beauty hath
Two forms

In the hidden wood, in
the room, sleep

Lady, who
art

FROM: "Epigon"

•

The earth the others
Call it darkling)
They flee. Persephone
Is never of their making, nor
Demeter. So
Women are delights,
things to run with, play, equals,
deers they slay

They only remember what space has had her arms around

(letter to FB, lines for Dahlberg)

["wizardess" he called his secret lover & Muse Frances Boldereff.]

•

To go to grass
As his daughter now suckles

We are blind
Not from darkness
But by creation we are moles. We are let out
Sightless, and thus miss
what we are given, what woman
is . . .

FROM: "The Death of Europe"

•

My vanity
Is only the exercise
Of my privilege as yours, conceivably,
Might be as heres, thye peahen, is
Also brilliant when she takes it up: Willendorf
The stone, breathes back
Into life.

FROM: "the chain of memory is resurrection"

Is it any wonder
My mother comes back?

•

(o mother, if you had once touched me
o mother, if I had once touched you)

Method, method
                    I call on you to come
                    To the aid of all men, to women most
                    Who know most, to woman to tell
                    Men to awake. Awake me,

    Awake

FROM: "As the Dead Prey Upon Us"

•

            Rise
Mother from off me
God damn you God damn me my
Misunderstanding of you
    ????

So the distances are Galatea

FROM: "The Distances"

In its entirety:

>   Cross-Legged.
>   The Spider and the Web
>
>
>   With this body worship her
>   If necessary arrange
>   To sit before her parts
>   And if she object as she might
>   Ask her for your sake to cover
>   Her head but stare to blindness
>   Better than the sun look until
>   You know look look keep looking until
>   You do know you do know

                          •

And, finally, from "Maximus"

>   " . . .to be on the sweetness of earth herself,
>   great goddess we take for granted . . ."
>
>>   —as the female animal in the boughs
>>   of the tree, out of eating the leaves makes milk
>>   which warriors do not know is
>
>   the initiation
>
>   of another kind of nation

the Blow is creation
& the Twist the Nasturtium

is any one of Ourselves
And the place of it ALL?

Mother Earth Alone

Coda:

What is the relationship between humans and Nature?

Homo sapiens sapiens — "Man, the wise, the wise?" Hardly.

Rather we seem planetary fools. Silly Olson w/goddess biz!

Atmospheric Chemist James Lovelock speaks of the relationship between
Humans and Nature as an "impending war." David Foreman wrote that
far from being the central nervous system of Gaia we are "a cancer eating
away at her."

The sperm tails of men evolved through symbiosis. There is a possibility
that sperm tails and oviduct *undulipodia* derived from Spirochete bacteria
that became ancestral cell "whips."

A discovery of *centriole-kinetosome* DNA on its own chromosome and
tightly packed at the base of each cell whip is the single most important
scientific advance for the theory of Symbiotic theory of cell evolution.
Remember DNA was only discovered in 1953!

In contrast to neo-Darwinian evolution as an unmitigated conflict in
which only the strong survive, there's an essential alternative to consider:

Charles Olson kissing his daughter Kate, Black Mountain College, North Carolina, 1952
PHOTOGRAPH COURTESY OF THE ARCHIVES & SPECIAL COLLECTIONS
AT THE THOMAS J. DODD RESEARCH CENTER, UNIVERSITY OF CONNECTICUT

An interactive view of the history of life on earth.

Recognizing ourselves not as lords but as partners. Olson intuitively was on to this.

SOURCES:
Olson, Charles, *Human Universe and Other Essays,* edited Donald Allen, University of California Press, 1965.

The Maximus Poems University of California Press, 1983.

Collected Poems, University of California Press, 1987.

Margulis, Lynn and Sagan, Dorion, *Microcosmos: Four Billion Years of Microbial Evolution,* University of California Press, 1997.

Neuralinguistically: This is the Writing Dance

This is the writing dance
Or a plumed helmet which itself
Resembles a heart in the shape of Africa · Continents! Continents!
The challenge is to question the "warrior"
Get inside his/her armor
Get inside the land which has no boundary
We could talk about China now
Its economics, its technocrats
The backdoor deals
We could happily be Canadian But could we really?
We could talk about Liberia, Suffering everywhere
& Congo & Lebanon and our own backyard
safe . . . starlit
Stomp on it right now
Out on that turf

This is the obsequious politician
Flattering you
You never believe him
Never. The eminence of philosophy
So crenellated, so terraced pronouncing
The name of your dance: Down with the tyrant!
That is the gesture and the name: Down with the tyrant
Down with his exaggerated thunder
You wanna talk psychosis?
Down with the tyrant
Daggers . . . hysterical puritans . . . starved animals

You wanna? You wanna? You want to talk?   You want to write?
        This is the writing dance, written   for all to see
                the whole picture of the decimated site, the picture
of charnel ground . . . the jackals came . . . & the jackals came
             sift, sift through the body parts
                          sift . . . sift . . .

      See the back of his head?
   Would a gesture   Knock him off?   Or is he too steely-eyed?
         Eyes look through the head — inside there the
              Little screen — the trick is to dance upon it
     The dance I was doing is the written dance
        To be a barker, be a noise maker, be a saint —
          Tools, linen, weapons, wires, women creating
             Sainthood, place hands together and bow
This was the written dance . . . eyes looking back on
themselves before growing cold, check out the moon
            Check out all the characters
The philosopher for example — her window of the room
The guy ready to blast his M16   The naturalist with razor gaze
       Dark streets out there below the moon?
Is that what I see?   Is it written? No this is the smitten dance
         Flying over the Occupied territories
      Don't talk to me about transgression any more
This is the trespass dance   This is the way I get down for it
       It's my power structure to strangle Rumsfeld!
           STRANGLE Rumsfeld!
    Avaunt thee thou Rumsfeld euphemisms!

    If I were a scientist I would scream in my
             Scientist voice   Neurons! Neurons!

I would say it again & again the way
the neurons like to be commended &
Commented upon: Dear Neurons
You can be kind   I would say elephants move like this
Neuralinguistically   Snakes move like that
Hyenas are shrieking at the body politic
If I were a Sufi I might spin outta control

This is not the terra firma dance
This is not the map of the capital materialist Junta dance
This is the writing dance   Ida Lupino liked it
She wanted the script to go on
Many of the women stars of another era
Were never confused about priorities
They had their stage directions. Their "moves"   Their maps
They had their "songs" their "gestures" their "postures"
They performed for a silver screen   They had their "desires"
Their sky was covered with a thin layer of clouds
Everything was quiet and still when they came on the "set"
It was like a scene of tranquil poetry
It was a scene you had to have been there for
As it got written   And the one who emerged, who lingered
Was the one you pointed to — was "she"
She who had been stalling, feet like the feet of many
Different animals   & with eyes in all the pores of their pelts
& voices   sounding as only she could as them,
and mapping
and changing the way the writing would go
if it were a dance
You might wonder

"Premises of Consciousness": Notes on Howl

every day is in eternity!
— ALLEN GINSBERG, *Howl*

Private Howl

The lineaments and landscape of *HOWL* when it hit the universe in the mid-late 1950's were familiar. I came to it, age 14. And I came to it again and again those early "coming of age" years. Having grown up on Macdougal Street, Greenwich Village, Manhattan, New York, daughter of bohemians, itinerant piano playing father turned educator by the grace of the GI Bill, mother who had spent time with her then father-in-law the poet Anghelos Sikelianos, Peter Seeger doing hootenanies down the block, folkies in protest in Washington Square Park (my older brother being one of them), Thelonious Monk I visited once with Steve Lacy (who was married to my former sister-in-law) not far away, struggling with heroin, school friends in all kinds of disarray (sex problems, drug problems, mental problems, pregnancy problem), the poem was an exhilarating and heartbreaking reflection of aspects and spirits of comrades of my own "naked," "raw," "artistic," "sensitive" personal life. I lived in my own howlesque subculture.

If you were odd, at all eccentric, you were Beat. My friends with knapsack of "Christ Climbed Down" and rolling papers, kids on junk, highschool girlfriend in a ward getting shock treatments. My own godfather closet gay, alcoholic, bedridden.

Andrea Dworkin, radical feminist was already doing an embedded stint in the Women's House of Detention when we were in high-school. My friend Martin Hersey (son of novelist John Hersey) had a copy of *Howl* and *Naked Lunch* in his raggedy guitar case. These were hip reader-ly reference points. My boyfriend was incarcerated in the Wingdale mental hospital. I would visit him, horrified at what I saw. I wrote tentative poetry:

> I am a bird over the Harlem Valley
> at Wingdale . . .

I knew "tenement roofs." I knew

> chained themselves to subways for the endless ride
> from Battery to holy Bronx . . .

> *(New York New York*
> *It's a wonderful town*
> *The people ride around in a hole in the ground*
> *The Bronx is up and the Battery's down)*

This was before "flower power," the rise of hippiedom, "Be In" glee, it was getting close to the civil rights push. I had friends going to Tent City in Mississippi by 1962. But before feminist and gay and lesbian movements, and psychedelics. Before AIDS, although maybe a prophecy of AIDS. Before the American War in Vietnam. Pre-French Structuralism. Before Lacan, Foucault, Derrida. Before the voyeurism of the culture industry.

But *Howl's* experience was also of the generation's before mine. Closer to my father's consciousness — being a male person drop out spell, jazz musician a time, smoker of weed. Going to Columbia in the late forties, suffering a kind of post-war trauma. This was the turf of the American psyche before the Vietnam War — still caught in the gray area post-WW II doldrums, a time constructed of false material promise. O those shiny

Nanao Sakaki, Anne Waldman, and Allen Ginsberg
in Prague after the Velvet Revolution, Czechoslovakia, 1990
PHOTOGRAPH BY JAROSLAV KRATOCHVIL

new gadgets that would make life easier and enhance family living, what illusion! How to escape? And how the cold war was to continue the dichotomy of this dangerous illusion.

Howl was decidedly written from a psychologically synergistic point of view which seemed highly referenced to the East Coast — specifically the New York City nexus. This made it immediately palpable. The underbelly evoked was "New York"— wild, phantom New York City, which is where Allen Ginsberg came to experience his streets at dawn, which became every street at dawn. In spite of reference to Denver and California and Kansas and Idaho and being composed in California, *Howl* carried the brilliant taint and power of New York City. It's on a cellular level this identity with this particular city. I felt that. I felt I was "in" on the sites of the poem. It was akin to my own experience, strange as that may sound as a very young female person.

The map of *Howl* was both microcosmic, macrocosmic. Of the particular, I had childhood friends we visited in Newark, summers to the Zen New Jersey Atlantic City shore, we celebrated birthdays in restaurants in Chinatown, Big Wilt Small's in Harlem was exotic, one engaged in romantic trysts on the Staten Island ferry, Empire State Building was where you brought out-of-towners, Third Avenue Elevated Railway "iron dreams" was iconic, rivers of the Bowery, yes they were surely running under our feet. I used to see Gregory Corso on this very Macdougal Street where I still sit writing. My father invited Allen Ginsberg to read at Pace University in 1959, a success. I had New York friends getting busted, shipped off to expensive mental hospitals — some exclusive like Riggs, or other houses of bedlam like Wingdale . . . and so on. Allen Ginsberg jump cuts all over the map but the reference point, the ur-point, the point of origin is New York City. This was the city that contained "multitudes," where any experience or combination thereof was possible. Where the races mingled, homosexual and lesbian persons had active spheres, where we had Commie friends and maybe my father was once a member of that party, I was never quite sure . . .

And *Howl* — perhaps most importantly as someone set on a path of poetry — was a monumental oral construct, more challenging and direct in its consciousness than "The Wasteland." You could hear its verticality projecting upwards/outward in the horizontal lines of "Moloch," in the "Holy" litany. The long breath lines outdid Whitman's, and created amazing film-like flickering *noir* montages of thrust and activity:

who wandered around and around at Midnight in the railroad
yard wondering where to go, and went
leaving no broken hearts,
who lit cigarettes in boxcars boxcars boxcars racketing through
snow toward lonesome farms
    in grandfather night

or

who sang out of their windows in despair, fell out of the subway
window, jumped in the filthy Passaic,
    leaped on negroes, cried all over the street, danced on broken
wineglasses barefoot smashed
    photograph records of nostalgic Europena 1930s German jazz
finished the whiskey and threw up
    groaning into the bloody toilet, moans in their ears and the
blast of colossal steamwhistles

It was a *cri de coeur,* an alarm, a vision. Its structure matched its energy
which seemed the voices of many, not one. It was a rhizomic collage, just
like life, a pastiche of the experiences of many others, encompassing flash-
es of "minute particulars." It was recognizing the first Buddhist Noble
Truth of Suffering which I was starting to hear about in my Comparative
Religion class at Friends Seminary, a realization that could trigger empa-
thy with the universe. How did one "do" this in a poem?

I could feel, viscerally, the possibilities this poem created for a contem-
porary poet — the permission it gave to an expansive poetics of our
time. Surrealist, cut-up, dream, documentation, aleatory strategies all
played in here. Whitman caught an America of a different time. A differ-
ent war. *Howl* was something both of the invisible America — an

Allen Ginsberg taking a photograph of Gary Snyder, Naropa, 1990
PHOTOGRAPH BY PETER COLE

America not discussed, not analyzed, fringe, "fellaheen," as Jack Kerouac would say — and the America that was facing the bottomless pit-reality of the atomic bomb that had already been dropped and might well be used again.

And there was my own obligatory rite of passage, traveling with my brother and a friend to California, site of the composition of *Howl* and hitching back from Mexico all the way to Manhattan. So 1965 I was in San Francisco, age 20, and although I had seen Allen close up, I missed his reading at the Berkeley Poetry Conference because my first LSD trip kept me from getting across the Bay Bridge. I could "feel" his pulse however. *HOWL* was already on the premises of my consciousness. We met later that week.

"The Breakthrough Thing" / "Unworldly Love"

I keep thinking I would like to be able to write another "Howl."
You know like taking the problems of the eighties, like ecology and
the Moral Majority, and all that. But you know you can't do that
deliberately, it has to come accidentally almost.
— ALLEN GINSBERG, *1989*

Allen in a lecture at Naropa University on July 4th, 1989, entitled
"Revolutionary Poetics," spoke thus:

The breakthrough thing. I experienced that with *"Howl"* —
a breakthrough, not of universal consciousness or the social
consciousness, but a discovery of my own consciousness, and
then a proclamation of that. I'm trying to lay it out on the page:
what is it I really desire. Instead of what I'm told I should know,
or desire.

•

Can you name what you desire? I took one key — from one line
in Williams: "Unworldly love, that has no hope of the world, and
cannot change the world to its delight."

•

So what eternal spring of feeling do you have in you, that you
feel sure of, or that you feel unsure of, but returns over and over
again, in dreams, and in waking moments of longing? What ob-

ject of love, or what desire, or what delight, returns over and over despite the appearances, despite discouragement, and despite all rational calculation — even trying to repress it, it still comes through. What freshness of feeling, and what freshness of perception, comes through anyway, even despite blocking it, even despite, either the condition of not noticing it, or thinking you better not do it (you better go straight, you better get a job) — what comes through anyway? What unworldly love, that has no hope of the world, and cannot change its world to its delight, persists, and breaks through always, if only in dreams? Because in dreams you get these great baths of eroticism or liberation or recognition. You know, your mother recognizes you, Kissinger recognizes you.

This sense Allen has of the discovery of his own consciousness with the making of *Howl* is what has kept the poem fresh, resilient. In fact it is the activation of the consciousness through the poem itself that is the key to its imprint in the world-poem-psyche. "Poetry is news that stays news" (Ezra Pound). *Howl* will continue to be a kind of rune for readers of the future. It carries what in Buddhism is called "transmission," which goes beyond literal historical time. It exudes a sense of immediacy, of discovery, of generosity. And what makes it seem more and more over time — like a sacred text, a sutra, a ritual that as it is read silently or aloud — is that it can be re-done, re-actualized, realized. The magnanimity of its reach never ceases. Its anaphoric "who," its lists of minute particulars, reverberate through time. It is a time machine, it is also a time bomb. It carries warning, prophecy. The desire or "eternal spring of feeling," its aspiration, is what drives its persistent existence.

Moloch

The visionary Moloch section, written while under the influence of peyote seems chillingly prescient. The Cannaanite fire god demanded parents sacrifice their children, a propitiatory ritual of auto-da-fe. We see the death toll of young soldiers in Iraq and Afghanistan rising, the untold deaths of countless innocent citizens of those countries and the ritual sacrifice made by teenage suicide bombers set to act by calculated ideologies, and the insult and humiliation they feel at the hands of the West. We send children to slaughter the world over, into the maw of the blood-thirsty beast.

Ginsberg references William Blake's Urizen in a footnote to Part II of *Howl*:

> the Jehovic hyper-rationalistic judgmental lawgiver Urizen, creator of Spiritual disorder and political chaos. His abstract calipers limit the infinite universe to his egoic horizon, a projection of unmindful self-hood, the result of aggressively naive mental measurements which substitute hypocrite or modish generalizations for experience of event, and oppress physical body, feelings and imagination.

This seems our human condition under the mind-set of Urizen who comes to symbolize all the tyrants of imagination and freedom.

Post 9/11, certain phrases seem especially apt to our current state of affairs in an Empire State driven by the vices of late capital — excessive greed, hypocrisy, and an ideology that thrives on a hallucination of a perpetual "enemy." A dark state of mind that doesn't nourish its many denizens — plant, animal, mineral — that prefers the "vast stone of war."

"Boys sobbing in armies"
"old men weeping in the parks"

"Moloch the incomprehensible prison! Moloch the crossbone soul
less jailhouse and Congress of sorrows! Moloch whose buildings are
judgment! Moloch the vast stone of war! Moloch the stunned
governments!"

"Moloch whose love is endless oil and stone! Moloch whose soul is
electricity and banks!"

"They saw it all! the wild eyes! the holy yells! They bade farewell!
They jumped off the roof! to solitude! waving! carrying flowers!
Down to the river! into the street!"

The image of human beings jumping off the World Trade Towers arises in
an ironic twist of time — searing in the eye's mind.

Outrider

And how did this poem epitomize what I've termed the "OUTRIDER" tradition since 1974 when Allen Ginsberg and I founded the Jack Kerouac School of Disembodied Poetics at Naropa University? The OUTRIDER holds a premise of imaginative consciousness. The OUTRIDER rides the edge —parallel to the mainstream, is the shadow to the mainstream, is the consciousness or soul of the mainstream, whether it recognizes its existence or not. It cannot be co-opted, it cannot be bought. Or rides through the chaos, maintaining a stance of "negative capability," but also does not give up that projective drive, or its original identity that demands that it intervene on the culture. This is not about being an Outsider. The OUTRIDER might be an outlaw, but not an outsider. Rather, the OUTRIDER is a kind of shaman, the true spiritual "insider." The shaman travels to zones of light and shadow. The shaman travels to edges of madness and death and comes back to tell the stories.

How "out" might you go from the strictures of official verse culture? From the thinking or the amnesia or the "denial" of the status quo?

Consider how Walt Whitman changed poetry from a very fixed and classical form to an open form anyone might participate in. Consider the ramifications in the political world, the social world, a world of defined gender and race and class. Consider the open field.

How might you ride your vehicle of poetry? How might you descend or ascend the map of your own imagination? How might you mirror the chaos you live in through a liberated and electrifying language?

Allen Ginsberg fought his whole life for the rights of free speech, for the unfettered, articulated power of the imagination. Even as he died, readings or recordings of *Howl* could not — and still can't — be broadcast on daytime radio in the United States of America. The struggle continues on many fronts. And one struggle is against the "institutionalization" of poetry, creative writing, of the imagination.

Allen had his own generation's terms and identifications. I felt — coming later — the need to define the ongoing hybrids of the New American Poetry lineage further, to include more women, and a more polysemous relationship to language and its "intentionality." To define the pedagogy of such a lineage so that it might flourish and continue, building on an ever-expansive poetics the concerns of the Black Arts movement, Black Mountain school, New York School, San Francisco Renaissance as well as — perhaps most importantly — the spirit of the Beat movement as it engages with, is able to inhabit, a larger public and oral space (as *HOWL* has been able to.) This poem has touched — and changed — many lives. Hearing Allen Ginsberg read it live was an event in eternity.

HOWL is still activated and re-created in many consciousnesses. *HOWL* plugs you into the socket.

HOLY 21st Century

Holy! Holy! Holy! Holy! Holy! Holy! Holy! Holy! Holy!
Holy! Holy! Holy!
Is the composite world holy? Holy phonemes holy neurons!
Holy the 5 senses! Holy the aggregates of being!
Holy impermanence! Holy the inter-connectedness of all beings!
Karma of atrocities holy and un-holy!
Is 21st century endless continuation of 20th century war holy?
Environmental degradation continuation
of 20th century environmental degradation holy?
Every Woman's a holy dakini! Matriot acts holy!
Holy! Holy! Holy! Holy! Holy! Holy! Holy! Holy! Holy!
Holy! Holy! Holy!
Body parts blown over the charnel ground holy!
Eyes ears nose hands mouth holy!
Manipulated Bible holy? Koran holy? Anarchist tracts holy? Fatwas holy?
Geneva Convention holy? Holy Contract with America,
come on citizens, is that holy?
Star Wars' "Rods from God" holy? Daisy cutters holy?
Thermobaric version of the Hellfire Missile that can turn corners
and blast into caves holy?
Allen's Ginsberg's "Mysterious rivers of tears under the sheets" holy!
Holy Kerouac's "tender reward!"
Holy Baghdad! Holy Dharamsala! Holy Columbine!
Holy Kabul! Holy Israel/Palestine! Holy Bosnia! Holy Rwanda!
Holy Manahatta Isle! Holy Trade Center! Holy East Timor!
Holy Justice! Holy forgiveness! Holy Truth! Holy Accountability!

Baghram holy? Guantánamo holy? Abu Ghraib unholy!

All hooded torture un-holy! All bodily sadistic harm un-holy!

All the hate un-holy! Big lies unholy! All the rape un-holy!

Unholy! Unholy! Unholy! Unholy! Unholy! Unholy!

Holy rap! Holy hip hop! Holy klezmer! Holy Afro-pop!

Holy jazz! Holy gamelan!

Holy pneumatic drills boring into the depths of Brooklyn!

Holy old slave graves!

False the military recruitment centers

knocking on tenement doors get a fresh martyr for!

Holy Creeley! Holy Lucia Berlin! Holy Jackson MacLow!

Holy Brakhage! Holy Carl Rakosi! Holy Philip Lamantia!

Holy Steve Lacy, blowing his saxophone in heaven!

Cloning holy? Stem cells holy?

Amphetamine holy? Un-holy the polarized universe!

Holy the unfettered Universe!

Holy Negative Capability! Holy No Ideas But In Things!

Holy Projective Verse! Holy Modal Structures!

Banish grief & greed

o compassionate green-skinned savioress of the Mind

HOLY OM TARA HOLY TUTTH TARA HOLY TURE SOHA!

SOURCES:

Ginsberg, Allen, *HOWL, Original Draft Facsimile, Transcript, & Variant Versions, Fully Annotated by the Author*, edited by Barry Miles, Harper & Row, 1986.

Ginsberg, Allen, "Revolutionary Poetics," in *Civil Disobediences: Poetics & Politics in Action*, edited by Anne Waldman and Lisa Birman, Coffee House Press, 2004.

Show You Out the Door

Manhattan's streets I saunter'd pondering . . .
—WALT WHITMAN, "Song Of Myself"

& I stay alive to look at things
& if I don't look at something beautiful at least once a day —
— go to the Metropolitan — see the Piero with well-dressed angels
down from Massachusetts, the
stunning newly-acquired Duccio infant feet symbolically at heart
— I go mad

But the box around the little painting shows your own reflection,
mortifying mirror
where is Virgin compassion (ho hum) in these hungry eyes?

paintings speak . . . traces . . . phonemes . . .
pink (another) on black with gold

Hungry eyes means "someone is looking"
Hungry person like you means you are "not just satisfied"
What is art but some hungry method or let down your voice
in this chamber you are supposed to be awed, wholesome
stop complaining about the glass, what these people keep in the
basement, what they are not showing us, museum as theme park

You will never be a rich person looking so strange
pacing the uptown galleries,
the Goya girl seems to follow you with her
eyes, the guard is approaching you
to show you out the door

I wanted to write a walking around poem
beginning with a trip to the Museum, Fifth Avenue was always wide
Was "Zone" influenced by Walt Whitman?
someone asked in Anselm Hollo's lecture class
in the distant school
which went from Apollinaire to Jack Spicer

Could the poets we love exist in one school?

Too passionate about art, poetry, modernism
You were young in it and you were walking these same streets
remember?

before you migrated . . .

Remember the girl couple — remember their embrace
One with dark hair, very tall, deep red fingernails
the other a gamin, pixie

"motion" "perspective" "random"

girls as "butch" as "femme" out in the world

too . . . passionate . . . about art, she said, sizing the other one (me) up

&

a fussy curator back inside (we were off the streets now)
said we were to be looking at the figure as if
from below okay we will try that & stay alive to try that
looking at her holiness from below, on my knees if you will

I want to touch it, her, art yes & you could be Walt Whitman
or Gertrude Stein anywhere in this town, revolving doors

Some of the thinking in here includes a metaphor of wolves,
hungry people,
the incarcerated, schools closing, sweet sense of being able to
turn a corner may be fallacious may be true

Turn

& I stay sensate to be loved & love you too and drag you to the heavenly
galleries where any civilization's artifact is free
you can just pay a nickel if you are a citizen
I will pay taxes to support this art but not war
(looking into that)

& love you freely and give you wide love that you could
travel anywhere in this love wide as it goes and it does to these steps
which take you away from the demonstration against an illegal war
you come inside & find some shelter here looking at things

& I started — me, an organizer, in love with poetry
— a school far from here
to consider "poetry as thinking" and it was
"beat" and it was lineage-conscious and it considered an endowed
Frank O'Hara Chair for a Poet of Deep Gossip and how we
might look at things amusedly, tragically, and talk about "lineage,"
"keep the world safe for poetry" etc.
& an Israeli Chair to be occupied by a Palestinian
& a Greek Chair to be occupied by a Turk
& Robert Duncan spoke at length that we could intuit reality

& we named a building "Allen Ginsberg" and wept and held memorials
when a poet dies, reading something aloud, holding books
with hands across the Rockies

& translation of these mental states

& this seems long ago . . . steps . . . founding a school . . .
archival glee . . . when we walked to the Museum
I couldn't get by without seeing something beautiful today
How many millions for a Duccio?
(worth it, she said)
& of course all the poets love a Piero
inestimable pleasure in a Piero

& consider the business of taxes we have to think of it's soon April
& consider the business of welfare how sad it goes
& consider the business of the end of nature
& the beginning & end of cities & Noam Chomsky
says we'll have suicide bombings soon on home turf
"Have you outstript the rest? Are you the President?"
said Walt Whitman

How they are laughing at us in Europe
Europe that we put in our Museums
How can we be a walking academy of trees
when we are tearing them down?

COLOPHON

Set in Bembo, a face by Monotype (1929)
based on the type cut by Francesco Griffo in 1495
for Aldus Manutius, master printer of Venice.
Stanley Morison named this revival after
Cardinal Bembo, whose book *Der Aetna* used
the original roman that this font emulates.
From the Italian Renaissance and its
pen nib stroke to the hot metal type
renaissance of the early 20th century,
Bembo's letterforms persist in
their clarity and elegance.

•

Book design by JB Bryan

Anne Waldman is the author of over 40 books and pamphlets of poetry,
including *Fast Speaking Woman* (20TH ANNIVERSARY, 1996); *IOVIS, Books
I and II* (1993 and 1997); *Marriage: A Sentence* (2000); *Vow to Poetry:
Essays, Interviews and Manifestoes* (2001); *Dark Arcana/Afterimage or Glow*
(2003); and *Structure of the World Compared to a Bubble* (2004). She is also
the editor of numerous anthologies including *The Beat Book* (1999);
co-editor of *The Angel Hair Anthology* (2001); and co-editor of *Civil
Disobediences: Poetics and Politics in Action* (2004). Her CDs include
Alchemical Elegy (2001); *Battery: Live At Naropa* (2003); and *The Eye of
the Falcon*, with Ambrose Bye (2006). She is an active member of the
Naropa University Audio Archive Preservation and Access Project.
With Ammiel Alcalay, she founded the activist coalition Poetry Is News.
Anne Waldman is co-founder of The Kerouac School at Naropa
University, and Chair and Artistic Director of its Summer Writing
Program. She also teaches part-time for the New England College
Low-Residency MFA program and is a founder, with Bob Holman
and others, of the Study Abroad on the Bowery program at the
Bowery Poetry Club on New York City's Lower East Side.
She has collaborated with many artists and musicians,
and has performed her poetry world-wide.